1

CourseBook Series

The CourseBook Series is the product of Dr. Mark H. Kavanaugh. Dr. Kavanaugh is a Professor of Psychology and Social Sciences at Kennebec Valley Community College. The CourseBooks contain the teaching content for each course.

Format

While definitively designed for digital distribution, each CourseBook is available in a number of formats. Distribution of the multi-touch ebook version is done exclusively through Apple Books. These CourseBooks may be purchased and downloaded directly to any iOS or Mac device.

Print versions of the CourseBooks are also available and are distributed through Amazon Kindle Unlimited.

Editing and Errors

Dr. Kavanaugh has written and edited all of this material but he is a horrible editor. He also cannot afford to have the work professionally reviewed. Mistakes, misspellings, broken links, and other errors may exist. Readers are encouraged to contact Dr. Kavanaugh directly to inform him of these errors for the next edition!

Copyright and Use

Dr. Kavanaugh owns the rights to the entire CourseBook. Others are free to use the CourseBook without permission. Graphics within the CourseBook are the original creations of Dr. Kavanaugh, downloaded from his Adobe Stock account, or are accompanied by attribution.

Index

Chapter 1 - The Study of the History of Psychology

Chapter 2 - Philosophical Influences on Psychology

Chapter 3 - Physiological Influences on Psychology

Chapter 4 - The New Psychology

Chapter 5 - Structuralism

Chapter 6 - Functionalism - Antecedent Influences

Chapter 7 - Functionalism - Development and Founding

Chapter 8 - Applied Psychology - The Legacy of Functionalism

Chapter 9 - Behaviorism - Antecedent Influences

Chapter 10 - Behaviorism - The Beginnings

Chapter 11 - Behaviorism - After the Founding

Chapter 12 - Gestalt Psychology

Chapter 13 - Psychoanalysis - The Beginning

Chapter 14 - Psychoanalysis - After the Founding

Chapter 15 - Contemporary Developments in Psychology

Special Assignments

- Article Summary
- History Timeline

How this CourseBook Works

The content of this CourseBook aligns with activities, expectations, and assignments that are found in the KVCC Learning Management System (LMS).

Students are expected to read and absorb the information in the CourseBook, read and review any textbook or other reading assignments, review the Assessment expectations outlined in each CourseBook Chapter, and participate in the expectations set by the instructor of the course in the LMS.

Chapter Organization

Each Chapter has been organized using an instructional design model called ALOTA, provides an outline of course materials that adheres to long-standing instructional design theory for adult learners. Namely, the model is greatly influenced by Gagne's Nine Events of Instruction

ALOTA

ALOTA is an acronym for the four essential parts of a lesson plan (or, in this case, chapter):

Attention
Learning Outcomes
Teaching
Assessment

Each Chapter in the CourseBooks series is organized in this manner in order to guide students through the material they are expected to learn.

Attention

Images, videos, text, and/or activities that bring readers into the focus of the lesson.

Learning Outcomes

Adhering to the language of Blooms Taxonomy of Learning Objectives, this section outlines the performance-based learning outcomes for the lesson. These align with the Assessment section of each lesson.

Teaching

This section can contain any variety of resources including text, lectures, recordings, videos, and links that provide a pathway through material to assist students in readying themselves for the Assessments.

Assessments

This section outlines assignments for students to demonstrate learning.

Additional Resources

Dr. K's Psychobabble

Dr. Kavanaugh also maintains a YouTube Channel called Dr. K's Psychobabble. You may find some of these videos embedded within this CourseBook.

Visit Dr. K's Psychobabble YouTube Channel

QR Codes

In order to ensure that readers of the print version of this CourseBook can still access online content, I have included QR Codes (such as the one listed here under my icon for Dr. K's Psychobabble.

Most smart phones are able to scan these codes with their camera and access the online material!

Apps in the CourseBook

Occasionally I will find mobile applications that relate to course content or are simply fun and engaging ways to learn. I will include links to these apps as the appear in the Apple App Store. It is likely that the same app is also available in Google Play but I will not usually provide the direct link to Google Play in the CourseBook.

Outcomes Alignment

Courses are designed to teach you a specific set of information and/or skills. These are largely determined by the specific learning outcomes through a course syllabus, in specific assignments and expectations, and in the structure of grading rubrics.

A course, however, often sits within a program that has learning outcomes associated with the expectations of external agents such as licensing board, accreditation, and other agencies.

This course rests in the Social Science / Psychology Department at Kennebec Valley Community College. The learning that is provided in this course is aligned with both the expectations of the American Psychological Associations guidelines for undergraduate Psychology education and with the Association of American Colleges and University's (AAC&U) VALUE structure.

This section provides you with information on how the learning activities (assignments, discussions, quizzes, etc.) align with the learning outcomes as designated by these external organizations.

Alignment With the Guidelines From the American Psychological Association

The American Psychological Association (APA) produces guidelines for the development of curriculum in the teaching of Psychology at the undergraduate level.

Here is a direct link to the document

The CourseBook series is designed to outline instructional materials and activities that demonstrate competence and knowledge in Psychology in alignment with these guidelines.

This section of each Psychology CourseBook will outline the specific content and activities (assessments) that align with the APA expectations.

Knowledge Base in Psychology

Describe key concepts, principles, and over arching themes in psychology.

- Chapter 6 Discussion - Darwin's Influence on Psychology.
- Chapter 11 Quiz - Respondent and Operant Conditioning.
- Chapter 12 Quiz - Gestalt Psychology.
- Chapter 13 Quiz - Relationship between Id, Ego, and Super Ego.
- Chapter 14 Quiz - Jungian Concepts.

Develop a working knowledge of psychology's content domains.

- N/A

Describe applications of Psychology.

- Chapter 2 Quiz - Mechanism as applied to Human Beings.
- Chapter 8 Discussion A - Learning about the Stanford-Binet Intelligence test.
- Chapter 14 Assignment - Using the Myers-Briggs Typology.

Scientific Inquiry and Critical Thinking

Use scientific reasoning to interpret psychological phenomena.

- N/A

Demonstrate psychology Information Literacy.

- Article Review Special Assignment.

Engage in innovative and integrative thinking and problem solving.

- Chapter 9 Assignment - Applying Classical Conditioning to Advertising.

Interpret, design, and conduct basic psychological research.

- N/A

Incorporate sociocultural factors in scientific inquiry.

- Chapter 3 Quiz - Experimental Psychology in Germany.

Ethical and Social Responsibility in a Diverse World

Apply ethical standards to evaluate psychological science and practice.

- Chapter 3 Discussion - The importance of Academic Freedom.

- Chapter 10 Discussion - Experiments

Build and enhance interpersonal relationships.

- N/A

Adopt values that build community at local, national, and global levels.

- N/A

Communication

Demonstrate effective writing for different purposes.

- Chapter 5 Discussion B - Describing

- History Timeline Special Assignment.

- Article Review Special Assignment.

Exhibit effective presentation skills for different purposes.

- Chapter 12 Assignment - Examples of Gestalt Perceptual Cues.

Interact effectively with others.

- N/A

Professional Development

Apply psychological content and skills to career goals.

- Chapter 8 Discussion B - Application of Psychological Testing to Careers.

Exhibit self-efficacy and self-regulation.

- Chapter 11 Discussion - Locus of Control and Attributional Style.

- Chapter 13 Discussion - Personal use of Defense Mechanisms.

Refine project management skills.

- History Timeline Special Assignment.

Enhance teamwork capacity.

- N/A

Develop meaningful professional direction for life after graduation.

- N/A

Alignment with the AAC&U VALUE Rubrics

In addition to the Learning Outcomes associated with the APA, specific to the field of Psychology, the Department has adopted additional learning outcomes as pretend in the structure of the VALUE Rubrics produced by the Association of American Colleges & Universities (AAC&U).

VALUE stands for "Value Added Learning for Undergraduate Education" and represents a national standard for the learning that should occur in undergraduate programs.

Below is a list of the specific expectations in this course that align with these outcomes.

Civic Engagement

- N/A

Creative Thinking

- Chapter 12 Assignment - Gestalt
- Chapter 14 Assignment - MBTI

Critical Thinking

- Chapter 1 Discussion - History
- Chapter 1 Quiz - History
- Chapter 4 Discussion - Introspection
- Chapter 5 Discussion A - Women
- Chapter 6 Quiz - Parsimony
- Chapter 7 Discussion - Darwinism
- Chapter 11 Discussion - Control
- Chapter 14 Assignment - MBTI

Ethical Reasoning

- Chapter 3 Discussion - Freedom
- Chapter 8 Discussion B - Decisions
- Chapter 9 Discussion - Animals
- Chapter 10 Discussion - Experiments

Global Learning

- N/A

Information Literacy

- Chapter 7 Discussion - Darwinism
- Article Review Special Assignment

Inquiry and Analysis

- Chapter 7 Discussion - Darwinism

Integrative Learning

- Chapter 11 Discussion - Control
- Chapter 12 Assignment - Gestalt
- Chapter 13 Discussion - Defenses

- Chapter 14 Assignment - MBTI

Intercultural Knowledge

- Chapter 2 Discussion - Dualism

- Chapter 3 Quiz - Experimental Psychology in Germany.

Lifelong Learning

- Chapter 2 Discussion - Dualism

- Chapter 8 Discussion A - Intelligence

- Chapter 11 Discussion - Control

Oral Communication

- N/A

Problem Solving

- Chapter 5 Discussion B - Describing

- Chapter 8 Discussion B - Decisions

- Chapter 9 Assignment - Behavior

- Chapter 11 Discussion - Control

- Chapter 12 Assignment - Gestalt

Quantitative Literacy

- Chapter 14 Assignment - MBTI

Reading

- History Timeline Special Assignment

- Article Review Special Assignment

Teamwork

- N/A

Written Communication

- Chapter 9 Assignment - Behavior

- Chapter 12 Assignment - Gestalt

- Chapter 14 Assignment - MBTI

- History Timeline Special Assignment

- Article Review Special Assignment

Interpersonal Communication

- Chapter 14 Assignment - MBTI

History of Psychology

This course focuses on the historical and philosophical roots of psychology and counseling. Topics include structuralism, functionalism, behaviorism, psychoanalysis, gestalt, and existentialism, as well as contemporary perspectives including evolutionary psychology, positive psychology, postmodernism, and feminist psychology.

This CourseBook is designed to be used with a companion textbook.

Schultz, D.P. & Schultz, S.E. (2011). *A History of Modern Psychology*. (10th Ed) Cengage

Changes made to this Edition of the CourseBook

1. New front material.

2. Updated outcomes alignment.

3. New author page.

4. Enlarged images when possible.

5. Chapter 3 - New video on deep brain stimulation procedure.

6. Chapter 3 - Added link to Chronicle of Higher Education article When Professors Offend Students

7. Modified Special Assignment - Article Review

8. General edits and clean up.

About the Author

Mark H. Kavanaugh, Ph.D.

Mark Kavanaugh has been writing, teaching, and integrating technology into instruction for decades. He holds a Masters in Counseling, Masters in Instructional and Performance Technology, and a Ph.D. in Educational Psychology. Mark lives in Maine with his wife Katie.

Visit Mark's Website

The Study of the History of Psychology

1

Attention

APA Division 26 - Society for the History of Psychology

The American Psychological Association is divided into a number of different parts representing focal points of research within the organization. Division 26 is the Society for the History of Psychology.

As a member of the APA, I became a member of Division 26 (additional money!)

Society for the History of Psychology

Learning Outcomes

Upon completion of this Chapter, students should be able to:

1. Describe what can be learned by studying the History of Psychology.

2. Discuss the challenges associated with accurate historical documentation.

3. Compare the personalistic and naturalistic views on the study of history.

Teaching

Why study the history of Psychology?

It might seem that modern ideas spring out of nowhere within creative people, but this is actually not true at all. Most creative people have spent a lot of time studying and knowing their field, they know what has been done, they appreciate the past, and now they are building on it to advance their field forward. This applies to nearly all of the creative activities of humans.

Jazz Music

For a short time, I went to college to study Jazz. I'm a bass player and I simply wanted to improve my playing. It was difficult for me to adjust to playing jazz music. To my ear, some of the notes seemed to not fit in with the chords and it sounded "wrong". I was assured that this was the point of the style of music. "Breaking the rules" is pretty much the expectation within the genre.

I loved this idea, I'm a rule-breaker by personality so I felt I had really found my genre of music. I could pretty much play what I wanted. When I did this, however, it sounded horrible. When my expert teachers and peers "broke the rules" it seemed cool and I could get what they were doing. When I did it, it simply sounded like I had not been playing for very long!

I can't remember which teacher it was who shed the light on this situation, but I was told something very profound: "In order to break the rules, you need to know the rules."

What I then discovered is that these talented jazz players understood the rules very well. They knew them so well, they knew where it was OK to break them and when it was not. That was the difference between their playing and mine. I didn't know the rules enough to know when it was OK to break them.

Applications to Psychology

While I'm still a musician, I have, for the most part, given up on the dream of worldwide fame. However, these lessons are applicable in my field as well. The new ideas in the field of Psychology are fascinating and amazing because they are built upon the collective history of the field. Researchers of new ideas are nearly always very aware of the history of research in their field.

In the very process of writing our work, the format requires that we review the preceding literature and provide an **historical** platform justifying why we chose to research in the direction we are going in. We will not discover anything new unless we have a clear indication as to what we have already discovered!

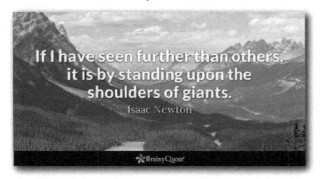

If I have seen further than others, it is by standing upon the shoulders of giants.
Isaac Newton

I have encountered a great number of creative students who have wonderful ideas. They have discussed with me their perceptions that their ideas have never been looked at before, that the field has ignored their specific perspective. Largely this is delusional. This does not diminish the idea, nor does it diminish the person. However, if this person wants to research in that particular area, they are going to have to do some leg work (reading, researching, writing) to find out what has already been found out.

Trust me, despite the existence of research on so many different things, there is always room for new ideas! Understanding where ideas have come from helps us to plot the path to new knowledge without repeating the mistakes of the past.

What do we mean by Modern History?

The approach in this course is to study the history of **modern** psychology. Psychology itself has its roots in the ancient world. We have been contemplating our existence and our thinking since we were first able to think, for thousands of years.

Our approach will be to look at the history of Psychology as a young science (only about 200 or so years old) when the first real scientists in the field borrowed the scientific method from Physics and Chemistry and defined what we know of today as the field of Psychology.

A lot of the history of this science is the effort to separate itself from the speculative aspects of its philosophical roots, and to define itself, through increasingly precise methods, as a science. Much of the history we will be exploring will encompass the history of the methods employed to study them!

Historiography

As with any field, the study of history has its methods. In this course we are looking at the field of Psychology, but we are really employing the methods used by anyone who is trying to document the past, particularly when no one who was there is still around!

Piecing together the history of Psychology is much like the work of an archeologist. The evidence often consists of fragments (letters, pictures, notes, journals) that are pieced together to create a picture of what it was like then. The artifacts of our history represent an incomplete collection. Items have been lost, edited, destroyed, suppressed, burned, hidden, embellished, fabricated, etc. etc.

We should not lose sight that, just like today, individuals edited the evidence of their lives to paint the best picture possible. This is more difficult today since it seems our history of ideas, expressed in emails, posts, and tweets, will never really go away and have a tendency to define us later on! In earlier years, the thinkers of the day had more control over the data available on them. The textbook describes some interesting instances of researchers destroying or modifying documents to produce a more favorable view.

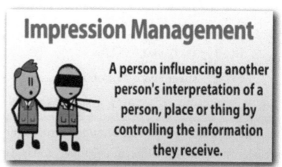

Impression Management

A person influencing another person's interpretation of a person, place or thing by controlling the information they receive.

Language Barriers

Another challenge to understanding history is language. Psychology is not a field that has been solely discussed in a single language. People all over the world study Psychology. As the field has been increasing its focus on cultural factors that impact behavior, it has to face the knowledge that translating work from one language to another can lead to significant changes in the original meaning of the writing.

The textbook example about Freud's concepts of the id, ego, and super ego is a great example. The German terms are more accurately translated into English as:

id = "it"

ego = "I"

super ego = "above I"

Though the difference is subtle, it is significant.

The term translated as "free association" actually meant "intrusion". Again, the different is subtle. Today we might think of "free association" as the experience we get when we are daydreaming. Our thoughts may move from one subject or memory to another rather freely and we are often surprised where it brings us.

This is not what Freud was after. He felt that the "it" (id) was actively intruding on the conscious of the "I" (ego). These intrusions indicated the needs of the "it" to meet its needs.

Bias

It is human nature to, in most cases, put our best impressions first. Psychologists are no different. We change data, we change our recollections, we change parts of the stories we tell...all to put ourselves in a more favorable light.

Consider the notion of a journal or a diary. It may be possible that you have a document somewhere that truly reflects your thoughts and struggles. What if you were under the impression that someday, maybe after you were gone, this journal would be published for others to see? Would you want that to happen? Would you even include some of the things that you wrote?

Most of us lead lives that will not attract the attention of biographers after we are gone so we don't have much to worry about. Then again, if we have a history of documenting our angst and frustrations on social media, could what we said years ago come back to haunt us later? Of course it can.

Not long after winning the coveted Heisman trophy, Oklahoma quarterback Kyler Murray, 21, found himself apologizing for tweets he sent as a teenager. A series of tweet of Murray calling someone "queer" resurfaced, causing a frenzy, despite it being roughly six years old.

Cultural Factors

Another set of factors that impacts history are the sociocultural and economic factors of the time and place. One instance of this is the emergence of applied psychology in the United States. Psychologists trained in Europe were not welcomed with open arms into the colleges and universities, so they applied their knowledge to industry (and the advertising industry was born!)

Struggling to legitimize the field (and get funding) Psychologists focused on practical solutions for existing problems. This does not seem like a "bad" thing, but it does take resources away from what we could call "purr research" which is the investigation of phenomena without a specific social good to come out of it. Pure research in Physics, for example, explores the nature of subatomic particles. The practical application of this may not be known, but the research for the sake of research and understanding continues. At the beginning, and often today, Psychology suffers from a demand to be practical and problem solving and that research should be focused in that direction.

This not only led to the field of Applied Psychology but it significantly impacted our understanding of basic human characteristics such as personality and intelligence. The money was to be found researching ways to address problems with personality and intelligence, not on simply discovering what normal personality and intelligence was.

Other sociocultural factors that had a significant impact on the direction of Psychology included:

1. The World Wars

2. Immigration

3. Discrimination (both the discrimination in our society and the discrimination within the field itself.)

Two Approaches to the Study of History

Our text outlines two basic approaches to the study of history. One, **Personalistic Theory** puts emphasis on the genius characters themselves. Essentially a study of the great minds of the field. The other is the **Naturalistic Theory** that presents social factors and key to understanding when ideas emerge into knowledge. Social factors actually "select" knowledge for publication because society is "ready" to hear that information. There is ample evidence that much research has been promoted to meet a social demand while other, possibly unpopular views and results, have been suppressed.

A science exists within its context (culture) and it adapts and changes just like any living organism would, when changes in that environment happen. The balance is how does the field change in response to culture and how much does it advocate for change in culture!

Moving Forward

As we explore the changes in the field of Psychology over time we will begin to appreciate that while there were strong voices that influenced the field (Freud, Skinner, etc.) there have always been those who disagree. The result is that Psychology has not necessarily had much of what we might call **paradigm shifts** because we have not had very many paradigms! The field can be thought of as a loose association of ideas, schools of thought, theories bound together through a shared methodology and curiosity.

That is why I became a Psychologist!

Assessment

This section describes the activities and assignments associated with this Chapter. Be sure to check with your instructor as to which ones you are expected to complete.

Note regarding Discussions: These activities are primarily geared toward students who are taking the course in either an Online or Hybrid format. It is expected that students will post an answer to the prompt contained in the section below and reply to at least two other students' posts in order to obtain full credit for the discussion. All posts must be substantive and contribute to the discussion.

Note regarding Assignments: These activities entail the creation of a "document" of sorts that needs to be sent to your instructor. Most of these may be papers. All papers must be submitted to the identified "Drop Box" for the assignment and must be in either Microsoft Word or PDF format. Pay attention to expectations such as title pages and APA formatting if these are indicated in the instructions.

Other assignments may entail different types of "documents" including presentations, artwork, charts, spreadsheets, and/or movies. Instructions on how to submit these will be included in the descriptions below

Though they will not be repeated, all of the above notes should be assumed in subsequent chapters, unless otherwise indicated.

Chapter 1 Discussion - History

We known that the documents that we use to create the stories of history are incomplete. Yet, we attempt to construct history none-the-less. How does this compare to the documents of your own personal history? Are there documents you would not want to see the light of day? How does your desire to leave a positive legacy compare to the efforts to edit the story of Psychology's history?

Chapter 1 Quiz

1. What can we learn from studying the history of psychology?

2. Describe the differences between personalistic and naturalistic conceptions of scientific history. Explain which approach is supported by cases of simultaneous discovery.

Philosophical Influences on Psychology

2

Attention

If humans are machines, can we build a better human?

We can see from the content of this chapter that the desire to build a thinking machine has been around for a long time. We continue to expand the world of computers to bring us closer to some semblance of artificial intelligence, if not "awareness" among the machines.

Science fiction has been taking this on for quite some time. Here are some examples:

Isaac Asimov's **Foundation** and **Robot** series. From this series we got the motion picture **I, Robot** starring Will Smith and his robot "partner" Sonny, who develops consciousness.

Also inspired by Asimov's books is the movie **Bicentennial Man** with Robin Williams. The movie explores the question as to how human does a machine need to become before we accept it as human.

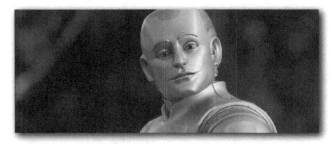

The movie **Ex Machina** explores the development of an android by an eccentric programmer. He recruits another programmer to determine if the android can make him believe it is human.

The test that Ava is subjected to is called the Turing Test (developed by the famed and tragic genius Alan Turing) that demonstrates if a machine can exhibit intelligence and actions that make them indistinguishable from humans.

Where are we now?

We continue to develop more and more complex computers to imitate human behaviors but we still seem to be pretty far from a true artificial intelligence that would pass the Turing Test.

What is AI - For People In a Hurry!

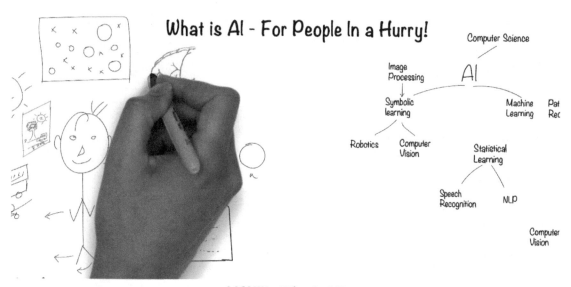

MOVIE - What is AI?

Let's get this straight...

According to the *The Telegraph* a super computer in Japan (the K computer, which is the 4th fastest in the world, was able to model the behavior of the human brain.

But here is the rest of the story.

1. The brain model consisted of representing the activity of 1.73 billion nerves connected by 10.4 trillion synapses (this is equal to 1% of our actual brain capacity!)

2. The computer has 705,024 processors and a whopping 1.4 million GB of RAM!

3. The computer was tasked with simulating 1 second of brain activity.

4. It took the computer 40 minutes to do it!

That 3-pound, soft jello-mold you have in your skull is an absolutely amazing powerhouse!

Read the article in The Telegraph

Learning Outcomes

Upon completion of this Chapter, students should be able to:

1. Explain the concept of mechanism and how it applies to a view of human beings.

2. Define and apply empiricism, positivism, and materialism and their impact on the development of Psychology.

3. Discuss the impact of Descartes' Dualism on modern day thinking.

Teaching

Mechanism

From the 17th to the 19th century society was deeply impressed by machines. Not only did we create clever machines, but they were also works of art. The root of this is that those who studied these things were felt there were exploring the very clockwork of creation. Such exploration should be adorned with beautiful art because they are exploring the work of God.

One of the most important, and most impactful, inventions was the clock. The precise measurement of time has profoundly impacted the psychology of human beings. Clocks were also considered models of the universe as a whole. The whole of creation was seen as a great clockwork. God was seen as a cosmic clockmaker.

This thinking created two philosophies that are still with us today. **Determinism** is the notion that there is a cosmic clockwork and that things are going to go along with the programmed mechanizations and we just need to leave it alone! The other philosophy, which dramatically effects our thinking is **reductionism**. This concept supports that if we understand all the working parts, we can understand the entire mechanism. Science has always been on the forefront of taking things apart to see how they work.

Later we will encounter the Gestalt psychologists who disputed this observation and coined the phrase that "the whole is greater than the sum of its parts."

People as Machines

It was not a huge leap for people to consider that humans were very much like the machines that they were inventing (we often see that today in way we describe cognitive processes using terms from computing...once again, our inventions teach us about ourselves!) Humans are just more complex!

As you can likely conclude, there are laws that govern the motion of machines and from this it was speculated that we could discover the laws that govern the behavior of humans. Thus the forward march of Psychology was to discover these "mechanical laws" for explaining human behavior.

Books and literature of the day reflected this sentiment. Hans Christian Anderson wrote about *The Nightingale* a mechanical bird, Mary Shelly wrote *Frankenstein*, and L. Frank Baum wrote about mechanical men and inspired the creation of *The Wizard of Oz*.

Thinking Machines

Although the animatronic world could create machines to imitate human movement, what about human thinking? Charles Babbage, fascinated with animatronics his whole life set out to build a thinking machine and ended up creating what is likely the first programmable computer.

Babbage Difference Engine - No. 2 -
Considered the first computer.

Although Babbage never stated that his machines were "thinking" he did not refute it either. He considered that his machines replicated simple aspects of the human mind and cognition.

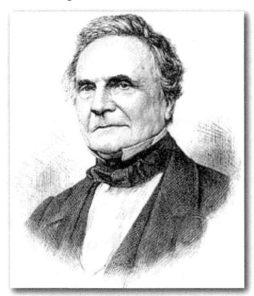

Charles Babbage (1791-1871)

Watch the machine in action!

Empiricism

Empiricism is the pursuit of knowledge through observation and experimentation. Not only was knowledge restricted to these processes, but it placed man in the center of the process of discovering truth without God. This was not only a forward movement of science, but a challenge to the prevailing thought that God was the only one who could understand the clockwork.

Descartes and the Mind Body Problem

Consideration of the relationship between mind and body had been going on for ages. Descartes wrote that he favored a much more significant role of the body. The mind can only think, all the other processes are found in the body. Things like reproduction, movement, and perception were seen as bodily functions and not a function of the mind. The mind has no material representation in this perspective.

Rene Descartes (1596-1650) - Image from Wikipedia

From here scientists accepted that the mind and body are two separate entities...we have been trying to get this couple back together ever since! This dualism has permeated nearly every aspect of our modern thinking. Even our own perceptions of our self are dualistic

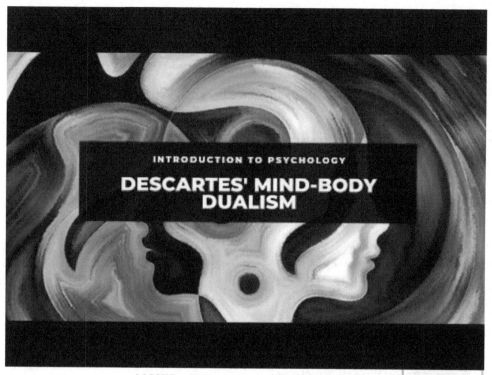

INTRODUCTION TO PSYCHOLOGY

DESCARTES' MIND-BODY DUALISM

MOVIE - Descartes Mind-Body Dualism

enough that we can say something like "me and my body", in some cultures this would see strange, they are one and the same.

The Doctrine of Ideas

Another important impact of Descartes thinking on the history of Psychology is the concept of **derived** and **innate** thoughts. Derived thoughts were considered to arise out of an interaction between the mind and the senses of the body. The result of some sort of external stimulus. Innate thoughts are considered those that arise from within the mind or consciousness.

It is particularly interesting to consider that many of the theories that would arise over the years in Psychology would battle of the prevalence of one of these over the other. Surely, Freud, for example would emphasize **innate** thoughts as the most important, Skinner, of course, would go for the **derived** thoughts. This duality of thought and perspective had multiple layers of influence and supports the notion of Descartes being one of the most influential Western thinkers ever.

Positivism

Auguste Comte (1798-1857)

Over the years, empiricism became so precise and produced such tangible results, that the philosophy about man's ability to solve his own problems began a life of its own. Positivism was the conclusion of Auguste Comte as he surveyed all the known science of the world and found that we (mankind) was no longer in need of dogma and spiritual/religious forces.

Another philosophy, **materialism** also gained ground. This perspective was that the universe could be described with science...again, no need for God. At this point the three prevailing thoughts centered around **empiricism**, **positivism**, and **materialism**.

John Locke

John Locke came along and took the idea of Descartes's dualism and considered the processes by which we think.

He supported that our ideas arise from two sources. One is derived from sensation while the other is derived from reflection. reflection is said to the source of ideas beyond the results of sensory perception...the imagination.

John Locke (1632-1704)

Our textbook provides a sample of Locke's own writing from his book, *An Essay Concerning Human Understanding*. This essay summarizes his important contribution to the field of Developmental Psychology, the concept of Tabula Rasa, or "blank slate". Locke considered the child's mind to be a blank page upon which experiences write the instructions. Children are born with nothing.

This is another great contrast in the world of Psychology. Some theorists emphasize the inborn qualities (genetic maybe) of a person , while other researchers focus on experiences and environment. This is the embodiment of the construct of **Nature vs. Nurture**.

Below is a short outline of some of the ideas of Locke and how the align with theories that we will see come into the world of Psychology much later.

1. **Simple ideas** (deriving from sensation and perception) and **complex ideas** (deriving from combinations of simple ideas) predicts the construct of developing **schemas** that will be put forth by Piaget. Piaget suggests that we start with simple schemas (ideas) and they become increasingly complex through interactions with the environment and the processes of **assimilation** (taking in brand new information) and **accommodation** (changing the nature of existing ideas to fit new facts.)

2. Locke's **Theory of Association** predicts the processes of **Classical Conditioning** (or learning). Classical conditioning operates on a premise of association between stimuli, like an object and a word, or an image and an emotional reaction. The result is that the two stimuli become connected.

3. Locke's concept of **primary** and **secondary qualities** of objects touches on the work do Piaget again. If you examine Piaget's stages of cognitive development you see the display of **primary**, **secondary**, and **tertiary circular reactions**. These mechanisms describe the development of internal representations of objects that children engage in through the first stages of their cognitive developmental processes.

George Berkeley (1685-1753)

Reading the story of Berkeley makes me want to go to more dinner parties so I can meet people who will give me money and make me financially independent!

Anyway...according to Berkeley, perception is the ONLY reality. This concept, later called **mentalism** purports that all we ever know is the product of perception. In some ways, there is no objective reality since all that we know passes through processes of perception. Berkeley's notion of **association of sensations** ties closely to Piaget's work mentioned previously.

David Hartley (1685-1753)

Hartley's concepts also likely influenced Piaget's work on cognitive development. Hartley felt that ideas or sensations that occur together become associated (classical conditioning) and **repetition** of these occurrences need to happen for these associations to happen (similar to Piaget's circular reactions...there is a repetition of processes that Piaget observed in children.)

James Mill (1773-1836)

In his singular work on psychology, *Analysis of the Phenomena of the Human Mind*, Mill purported that the mind was nothing but a machine. That subjective experience did not exist. James Mill was a strong believer in Locke's concept of Tabula Rasa, and was determined to determine what experiences would be written on to his son's mind!

John Stuart Mill (1806-1873)

The son of James Mill, John grew up in a demanding household with little love. Despite this severe upbringing and a mental breakdown, J. Mill would grow to fall in love and marry Harriet Taylor who would have a tremendous impact on his life.

Mill published an essay titled *The Subjection of Women*, in which he expressed notions of equality between the sexes, that women should not be forced to have sex, that they should have financial freedoms and rights equal to men, and that divorce should be granted on the grounds of incompatibility between two equals. He was a bit ahead of his time!

Mill is most famous for his contention that the mind is deeply involved in mental processes of information. He felt the mind could combine different ideas to create entirely new ideas, a process that later became known as **creative synthesis**.

Assessment

Chapter 2 Discussion - Dualism

Consider the ideas of Descartes' Dualism. From this we developed the divide between mind and body. In today's world, we see a concerted effort to rejoin the mind and the body and a deeper realization as to how each influences the other. Share your thoughts about the relationship between your mind and body. Feel free to research topics such as nutrition, exercise, health/illness, etc and its impact on the mind.

Chapter 2 Quiz

1. Explain the concept of mechanism. How did it come to be applied to human beings?

2. Define positivism, materialism, and empiricism and what contributions did each viewpoint make to the new psychology?

Physiological Influences on Psychology

3

Attention

So, if I hit my head and it swells up, will I be more intelligent?

Franz Joseph Gall developed the notion that the shape of the brain, reflected in the shape of the skull could be used to determine the degree of function in that area. This was not illogical, he had already observed that animals with larger brains could produce more complex behaviors. It stands to reason that if specific areas of the brain we larger, these functions would be enhanced.

The mapping of the skull became known as **Phrenology** and it remains one of the most quirky incidents in the history of Psychology!

Phrenology quickly took off and people were getting the shape of their skull documented by the thousands. Research indicating that the shape of the underlying brain did not correspond with the shape of the skull did not seem to dampen the enthusiasm.

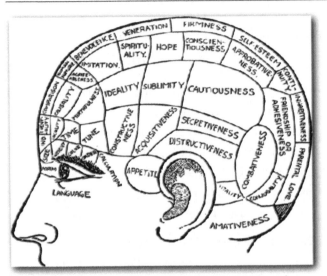

Map of specific locations of abilities according to Phrenology -

Image from Tincture

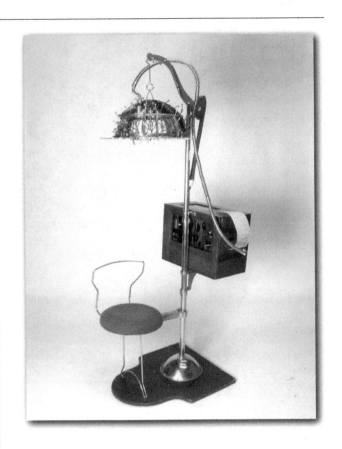

RARITY № 15320
c. 1830

PSYCHOGRAPH

PHRENOLOGY MACHINE USED

TO ANALYZE THE BRAIN.

Rogers Rarities

MOVIE - Explore the use of the Phrenology Machine

Learning Outcomes

Upon completion of this Chapter, students should be able to:

1. Describe the factors in Germany that made the development of Experimental Psychology possible

2. Describe the methods that scientists used to map brain functions.

3. Discuss the importance of academic freedom and public debate.

Teaching

Research on the Brain

Methodologies began to develop that allowed us to begin research on the physiological aspect of our being, the brain and nervous system. Here scientists began to appreciate that certain physiological aspects of our bodies impacted the way we perceived things. The mind-body was not dualistic!

Extirpation

The effort was underway to map the functions of the brain. Casual observations was not enough so a method was developed by Pierre Flourens (1794 - 1867), where one would remove or destroy parts of the brain and observe behavior in order to determine the function of that part of the brain. This, of course, was done on animals, not people.

Pierre Flourens (1794-1867)

Clinical Methods and Brain Stimulation

Paul Broca (1824 - 1880) performed an autopsy on a mental patient who was unable to speak intelligibly and discovered lesions in a specific area of the frontal lobe of the cortex. He concluded that this area of the brain had something to do with speaking. That area is now called **Broca's Area**.

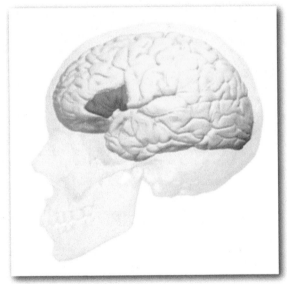

Broca's Area

Another methodology involved the direct electrical stimulation of the brain. Researchers were able to map the areas of the brain and the parts of the body they were responsible for. Direct electrical stimulation of the brain in patients who are undergoing brain surgery is critical for locating specific areas of the brain. Yes, you read that right, patients of some brain surgeries are kept awake so that they can report their experiences when parts of their brain are stimulated!

MOVIE - Deep Brain Stimulation at Michigan Medicine

Research on the Nervous System

Luigi Galvani (1737-1798) was the first to suggest that the nervous system sent electrical impulses. We see Galvani's name repeated in tribute to his work with electricity in industry and psychology. The **galvanic cell** is a type of battery, we use electricity to coat the outside of metals through a process called **galvanization** which produces rust-resistant **galvanized metals**, and the measurement of the electrical conductivity across the skin, a tool used in biofeedback and stress reduction treatment, is called **galvanic skin response**.

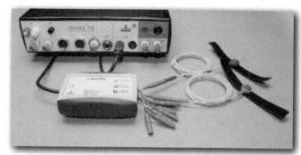

Measuring Galvanic Skin Response using the iWorx Lab System

By now we know that the nervous system communicates with electricity and is made up of many small parts (neurons) and that these neurons for connections with each other (synapses.)

Research then took a turn into understanding the mechanisms of the nervous system (a return or reinforcement of the mechanistic spirit).

The Birth of Experimental Psychology

A lot of people were curious about Psychology, but why did experimental psychology get its start in Germany? Mostly this was because experimental physiology was already well established in Germany and German temperament was well suited to the work of precision and classification needed.

Another factor was the sweeping reform that took over German universities that encouraged Professors to teach whatever they wanted without any outside interference. This laid the foundation for a flourishing research environment and is the core ethic related to "academic freedom" that we have in today's colleges and universities.

Sadly, this ethic is under attack with the advent of perspectives of progressive thinkers that educators should be sensitive to the emotional needs of student. Material that students may find "offensive" should be excluded and suppressed because this experience has been categorized as a micro-aggression. I cannot imagine a more ridiculous sentiment!

While I agree that academics should be taught with scientific rigor, the very purpose of higher education is to provide experiences that challenge current perceptions. College SHOULD leave you uncomfortable. This does not need to be mean spirited, but it is the only way to teach essential critical thinking skills.

When Professors Offend Students

To view this article you need to sign up for a free account

Johns Hopkins University (1876) was the first University in the US to support active scientific research. It was designed under the German model.

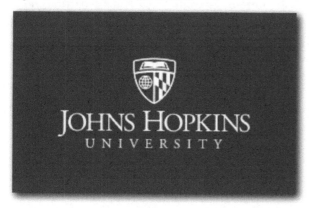

According to John Dewey, students and teachers from Johns Hopkins would meet to drink German beer and sing German songs! I'm fairly sure that John Hopkins continues to support both research and beer drinking to this day!

Below we are going to go through some of the great names in German Experimental Psychology.

Hermon von Helmholtz (1821-1894)

Image from Wikipedia

1. Studies physics, physiology, and psychology.
2. Invented the ophthalmoscope for examining the eye.

3. He published extensively on optics.

4. Researched the speed of the nerve impulse, reaction time, and how muscles focus the eye.

Ernst Weber (1795-1878)

Image from Wikipedia

1. Studied the sense organs, in particular, skin and muscular senses.

2. Introduced concepts to define sensation and perception including the **two point threshold** (how far apart two stimuli need to be to be detected as separate on the skin) and **just noticeable difference** (the degree to which a stimulus needs to change so that the change is noticed.)

3. **Weber's Law** established that sensory events can be related mathematically to measurable relative changes in physical stimulus values.

Gustav Fechner (1801-1887)

Image from Wikipedia

1. Studies sensation and determined the concept of **absolute threshold** (the smallest amount of stimulus that can be detected by our sense organs.)

2. Similar to **just noticeable difference**, he came up with **differential threshold** (how much change in stimulus to produce a change in sensation.)

3. Introduction of **psychophysics** (the study of the interaction between the physical and mental worlds.)

Examples of Absolute Thresholds

1. **Vision** - The amount of light present if someone held up a single candle 30 mi (48 km) away from us, if our eyes were used to the dark. If a person in front of you held up a candle and began backing up at the rate of one foot (30 cm) per second, that person would have to back up for 44 hours before the flame became invisible.

2. **Hearing** - The ticking of a watch in a quiet environment at 20 ft (6 m).

3. **Taste** - One drop on quinine sulfate (a bitter substance) in 250 gal (946 l) of water. Quinine is one of the components of tonic water.

4. **Smell** - One drop of perfume in a six-room house. This value will change depending on the type of sub-stance we are smelling.

5. **Touch** - The force exerted by dropping the wing of a bee onto your cheek from a distance of one centimeter (0.5 in). This value will vary considerably depending on the part of the body involved.

Assessment

Chapter 3 Quiz

1. For what reasons did experimental psychology emerge in Germany and not elsewhere?

2. Describe the early methods that scientists developed to map brain functions.

Chapter 3 Discussion - Freedom

In this Chapter, I reflect on the importance of academic freedom and factors that currently challenge this freedom. Discuss your thoughts on how challenging topics should be dealt with in the classroom. Share any experiences you may have had regarding how this was done well, or poorly.

The New
Psychology

4

Attention

Can we attend to more than one thing at a time?

This is the question that inspired Wilhelm Wundt, the Founding Father of Modern Psychology! Can we truly multitask?

Defining Multitasking

1. Performing two or more tasks at the same time.

2. Switching back and forth from one thing to another.

3. Performing a number of tasks in rapid succession.

Multitasking has been seen as a way to become more productive and to get more done. The results of research does not support this conclusion. The cognitive processes that need to happen for multitasking include:

1. **Goal Shifting** - deciding to one thing instead of another.

2. **Role Activation** - changing from the "rules" of the first task to the "rules" of the second task.

Here is what we know

1. People lose time when they switch from task to task.

2. People perform tasks slower when they have to switch from one to the other, and this increases with the complexity of the task.

3. Heavy multitaskers have less ability to sort through information, even when they are not multitasking.

4. Spreading attention across multiple stimuli impacts the person's ability to remember things.

Keep this in mind, this does not include the practice that some people have of keeping the TV (or music) on when they are studying. The multitasking here includes to active cognitive processes like...ummm...listening to a lecture and texting!

Two great Resources

Cherry, K. (October 30, 2018). How multitasking effects productivity and brain health. Accessed from www.verywellmind.com on January 13, 2019.

Carr, N. (2011) *The Shallows:* What the Internet is Doing to our Brains. W.W. Norton & Company

Learning Outcomes

Upon completion of this Chapter, students should be able to:

1. Discuss the use of Introspection as a primary tool for investigation of psychological phenomena.

2. Discuss the results of a typical Thematic Apperception Test.

Teaching

Wilhelm Wundt (1832-1920)

Wilhelm Wundt

Wundt is considered the Father of Modern Psychology. He has this distinction for the following reasons:

1. He was the founder of Psychology as a formal academic discipline

2. He established the first Psychology laboratory.

3. He edited the first journal of Psychology

4. He began Experimental Psychology as a science.

That is a pretty good list of accomplishments!

One of the accomplishments of Wundt that ushered him into the lofty role of "Father" of Modern Psychology was the fact that he successfully "sold" the idea of Psychology as a "science" to the world of science! (Which, of course, means that up until that time, most sciences did not consider Psychology worthy of study!)

Experimental Psychology

Wundt focused a lot of his work on trying to understand the relationship between the mental and material world. His laboratory used various instruments in his pursuit to define, scientifically, the processes of sensation and perception.

A description of the different apparatus present in Wilhelm Wundt's Lab in Liepzig

Cultural Psychology

Cultural Psychology was another area of interest for Wundt. This was the precursor to Social Psychology and it was important because it divided the field of Psychology into two separate disciplines, Experimental Psychology and Social Psychology.

Brilliantly, Wundt concluded that while the simpler physiological responses demanded a rigorous scientific approach of study, higher mental functions such as learning memory are not fit for that approach because of the complexity of language and other aspects of our culture. It would be better, according to Wundt, to ap-

Chronoscope

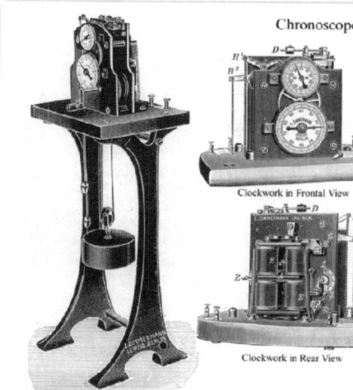

Clockwork in Frontal View

Clockwork in Rear View

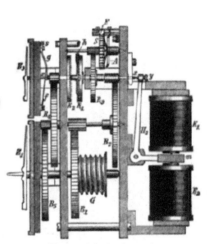

Clockwork in Sectional View

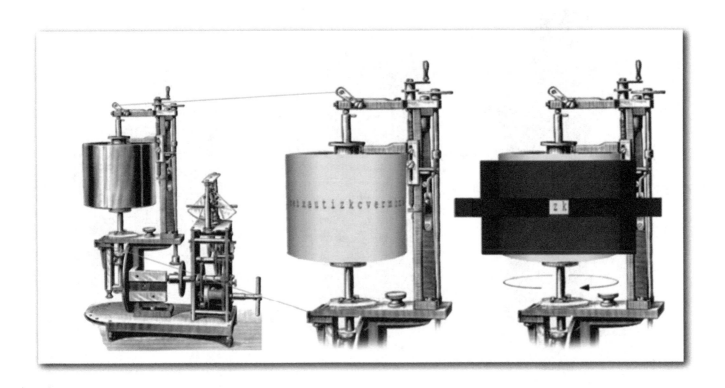

MOVIE - Brass Instruments of Psychology

Although the instruments in this video predate and postdate Wundt, it is an interesting presentation on the types of instruments that were constructed at the beginnings of Experimental Psychology.

proach these areas with the tools available in Sociology, Anthropology, and Social Psychology.

It is compelling for me to consider this early distinction. Our generation of psychologists is very focused on quantitatively analyzing some of these very areas that Wundt felt were not subject to such methods. Education, for example, is focusing more and more on "measurable results." While this, in and of itself, is not such a problem, we might be missing the more nuanced aspects of a complex process like this. Do we really walk away from a class having only learned the things on the test? Don't we learn much more about interacting with others, personalities of the teachers and students, methods of studying, etc.

With the focus on quantitative and numerical analysis, we might be ignoring some of the most important aspects of the learning process.

The Study of Conscious Experience

Much of Wundt's work was, in fact, the study of consciousness. Wundt felt that the mind was adept and bringing various stimuli together and constructing

meaning from them. (Wundt really places himself as one of the first Constructivists thinkers, the concept that we actively construct our reality.)

Wundt contrived the term **voluntarism** to describe the conscious will to organize the mind's content into higher-order thinking. He also focused on **immediate experience** (versus what he called **mediate experience** - information that we have about an experience aside from the experience itself.) This focus was definitively focused in the immediate, here-and-now.

Introspection

Since Wundt was focused on the conscious experiences that people had, this could not be directly observed by instruments (the instruments were designed to create and measure the experiences.) Researchers had to engage in introspection and contemplate/study their own experiences, one's own mental state.

Creating conditions that would render this process more objective (there is not much experience we can say is more subjective than introspection) Wundt required that the instruments that were used were very specific and accurate, and he required his associates to have a tremendous amount of experience in self reflection. According to our book, they had to have engaged in 10,000 introspections before the data they collected could be used in Wundt's lab!

Just to put that in perspective. Let's say I want to be an experimenter in Wundt's lab and I've given myself 5 years to get there. Not counting weekend there are 260 days (261 on a leap year) in a year. In my 5 year period there will be one leap year, giving

me a total of 1301 days. To be ready to work in Wundt's lab I would need to compete over 7 introspections every day for 5 years!

Elements of Conscious Thinking

Wundt outlined a couple of the elements of conscious thinking and Consciousness. Today we include other aspects of consciousness including memories, expectations, and cultural aspects of the situation.

1. Sensations - classified by intensity, duration, and sense modality (vision, hearing, etc.)

2. Feelings - the tridimensional features of "feelings" included 1) a subjective feeling of pleasure or displeasure, 2) tension, anticipation and relief, and 3) excitement and depression.

Wundt described the process of combining the disparate elements of consciousness into a creatively synthesized whole. He called this process **apperception**.

It is interesting to consider that in the field of Personality, there is a test called the TAT, or Thematic Apperception Test. The test is used to evaluate a person's personality by having them look at a vague picture and tell a story about the picture. You can see how this is an application of this creative synthesis process. Based on the type of story someone comes up with, the attending psychologist can evaluate the person's personality.

Typical Thematic Apperception Test Card

Assessment

Chapter 4 Discussion - Introspection

Wundt advocated for the use of introspection as a primary research tool. Discuss the validity of this method. Consider, as well, the preparation that Wundt demanded from his researchers. Would this make a difference?

Chapter 4 Quiz

1. View the image from the Thematic Apperception Test. Write your own story about what you think is happening in the picture.

2. Provide an introspective analysis as to what YOUR interpretation of this picture may say about you.

Structuralism

5

Attention

Building Blocks of Consciousness

Both Wundt and Titchener were interested in deconstructing cognition and conscious experiences. Sort of like a person might take apart a machine and examine all it's parts in order to understand how it works.

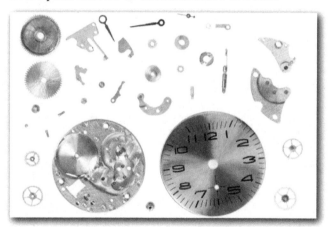

Remembering our "clockwork" conversation, the image above includes all the parts to a watch...you can understand how the watch works when you examine each part and its relationship to the rest...and, put together properly, the working watch is a sum of its parts.

One of the critiques of Structuralism is that the whole mind is more than the "Sum of its Parts"

MOVIE - Movie on Wundt, Titchener, and Structuralism

Learning Outcomes

Upon completion of this Chapter, students should be able to:

1. Evaluate Titchener's contribution to the role of women in professional Psychology.

2. Apply Titchener's method of objective description to a familiar object.

Teaching

Titchener and Structuralism

Edward Bradford Titchener (1867-1927)

Different from the work of Wundt, though introspective in method, Titchener felt that the focus of Psychology should be on the basic mental elements discarding the notion of apperception. This basic elemental view would later be a large part of the behaviorist perspective in the US.

Titchener and Women in Psychology

The book does a tremendous job on examining Titchener's curious approach to women in Psychology. While he promoted women in doctoral programs, supervised their research, and advocated for their assignment to faculty positions, he still did not admit them to the "club" of Experimental Psychologists that he created. What a strange dualism associated with this set of facts!

Your book mentions that Cornell University has a collection of brains including Titchener's. This is true and it is part of a collection of brains at Cornell.

Visit the Brains of Uris Hall at Cornell!

The Content of Conscious Experience

Titchener recognized the subjective nature of the study of psychological experience and how it differed from the subject matter of other sciences.

While he was as rigorous as Wundt in terms of preparation for introspection, he demanded that observations be made very objectively, describing the stimulus rather than making what he called, a **stimulus error** by naming the object.

Most of us would describe this as an "apple" but to do so would be a violation of Titchener's expectation to be objective. Consider this description...

"What I see is a mostly round object, with an outer coating of various shades of red. At the top of the object is a small thin appendage. The appendage attaches to the object at the bottom of aa slight depression. Attached to this appendage is another very short appendage which then widens into a flat surface, tapered at the end attached to the first appendage and at the distal end of the appendage. Water droplets have accumulated on the outside of the object, aggregated mostly at the top of the object with some sliding down the side."

The Elements of Consciousness

Titchener proposed three essential problems associated with the study of Psychology

1. Reduce conscious processes to their simplest components.

2. Determine laws by which these elements of consciousness were associated.

3. Connect the elements with their physiological conditions.

Consciousness was defined with three components: sensations, images, and affective states. Sensations refer to those things that are picked up by the sensory system, images are more like the ideas (imagination, maybe?), and affective states are the emotions. He also felt that we could describe our experienced with sensations, images, and affective states using the following criteria:

1. Quality is the characteristic that distinguishes the mental element from others.

2. Intensity refers to the mental element's relative weakness or strength.

3. Duration is the experience over time.

4. Clearness refers to the role of attention to conscious experience.

Interestingly, the book says that while sensations and images have all four of these, affective states only have the first three. I would imagine that the degree to which we attend our affective state is not only a part of our consciousness, but a critical element of it. It is the basis of such constructs as Emotional Intelligence.

Assessment

Chapter 5 Discussion A - Women

Review the history of Titchener's values and actions in regard to women in Psychology. Discuss how a person might be able to hold such contradicting values. Why do you think Titchener could both promote women in the field but yet continue to exclude them from his "club" of Experimental Psychologists?

Chapter 5 Discussion B - Describing

Select a common object in your environment. Provide a picture of the actual object, its name, and then provide an objective description. Have fun with this one! Who can come up with the most intense and descriptive statement?

Functionalism: Antecedent Influences

6

Attention

"Survival of the Fittest"

While we often attribute the phrase "Survival of the Fittest" to the work of Charles Darwin, it was actually NOT Darwin who coined this term. "Survival of the Fittest" was a phrase coined by **Herbert Spencer** (1820-1903) after he had read Darwin's work and applied the concept of Natural Selection to economics!

Spencer's use of the phrase has led to the application of the concepts of evolution, natural selection, and other ideas from Darwin in a diverse number of fields. Nations themselves, deemed to be more "fit" than others may be seen as surviving conflict and thus that culture will continue to propagate itself, while less "fit" societies will disappear.

Spencer of often thought of as the creator of a concept titled **Social Darwinism**. Social Darwinism is the application of Natural Selection to human societies.

Herbert Spencer

MOVIE - Misunderstanding Evolution
A Historian's Perspective on Social Darwinism.

We will learn more about Spencer's application of Darwin's thoughts to societies in the next chapter!

Learning Outcomes

Upon completion of this Chapter, students should be able to:

1. Discuss the important impacts that Darwin, and the Theory of Evolution, had on the study of Psychology.

2. Outline the limitations imposed by the application of the Law of Parsimony.

Teaching

The Impact of Darwin

We would be hard pressed to come up with a more influential character in science. Darwin's work, in particular his famous book *On the Origin of Species* transformed all the natural sciences and provided a framework for understanding the origins of our world, and of ourselves. In the world of Psychology he transformed the focus of study from structure (what are the parts) to function (what are they for.) You see, with evolution and natural selection now in play, our behaviors, as bizarre as they may be at times, were surely selected by nature and enhanced our survival as a species. Psychology began to see behavior in the light of adaptation to changes in the environment that would benefit the individual and the species as a whole.

Decidedly an American initiative, **Functionalism** was an approach to Psychology that directly opposed and protested against Wundt's **Experimental Psychology** and Titchener's **Structuralism**. The focus was now on how behavior helps people adapt to situations. A new age of Psychology was dawning as it began to apply knowledge toward specific problems. This was the beginning of what we know of today as **Applied Psychology**.

Charles Darwin (1809-1882)

Although the idea of evolution (that organisms change over time and pass on these changes to the next generation in response to the environment) has been around for a long time, Darwin was the individual who gathered enough information and data from his journeys that the scientific world could no longer avoid dealing with his theories.

Visit Darwin Online to access all his Books, Papers, and Letters

Darwin's impact on Psychology was particularly felt with the publication of *The Descent of Man* in which he argues that mental capacities and emotional reactions in humans are the residuals of functional behaviors on the part of our animal ancestors. These mental capacities, in their original form, must have served a function for survival in order for them to be passed on through so many generations.

Read Darwin's "Biographical Sketch of an Infant"...an important influence on the world of Developmental Psychology.

Darwin's Impact on Psychology

To summarize the impact of Darwin's work, and others that followed and supported him, it can be said that Psychology developed:

1. A focus on animal psychology, which formed the basis of comparative psychology.

2. An emphasis on the function rather than the structure of consciousness.

3. An acceptance of methodology and data from many fields.

4. A focus on the description and measurement of individual differences.

Each of these has had tremendous impacts on the direction of Psychological study.

Individual Differences

One aspect of the application of Evolution to Psychology was the focus on individual differences. This represents the slight changes in an individual's make up that may or may not be an adaptation to the environment. Being able to measure these differences became a key focal point in the world of Psychology.

Francis Galton (1822-1911)

In his book *Hereditary Genius*, Galton outlines that he could not accept that environmental factors were enough to produce the diversity of intelligence. He proposed that this characteristic was hereditary. His passion to encourage intelligent and gifted people to have children and for those of letter abilities to refrain led to the development of the science of **eugenics**. He felt that through selective child-bearing, the status of the human race could be made better.

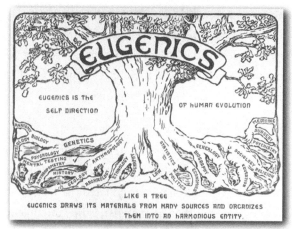

Eugenics, when it was translated to America, was an inspiration for Nazism.

Galton professed that genetics provided a maximum capacity for the development of all sorts of traits and that this genetic endowment was the more important quantity that predicted ability. Despite the efforts of schools, or exercise, or opportunity, heritability ultimately set how high someone could go.

Statistics

Adolph Quetelet (1796-1874) established the use of statistical calculations and the "normal curve" to describe human characteristics such as height. Galton was fascinated by this application and felt that it would be an excellent tool in the development of instruments to measure human mental abilities.

It is Galton who suggested that the measure of any trait across a large number of individuals would approximate the normal curve. He felt that two numbers could essentially be used to describe how traits vary across large populations, the mean, or average, and the dispersion (standard deviation.)

Galton went even further and suggested that because these measures produce standard distributions (normal curve) this data could be used to calculate the relationship between two factors. Galton gave the world of

Psychology one of the most powerful tools still used today...the **Correlation**.

Karl Pearson (1857-1936)

Galton observed that specific characteristics, when tracked across generations, tended to regress toward the mean. Over time the variance of a trait reduced. This methodology was picked up by one of Galton's students, Karl Pearson, who developed the statistical analysis of correlation called the **Pearson Product Moment Correlation Coefficient**, or simply, **r** (which is the first letter in the word "regression.")

Mental Tests

Although history attributes the term "mental tests" to James McKeen Cattell (1860-1944), an American psychologist, it was Galton who originated the idea of mental testing. He felt that characteristics like intelligence could be measured using specific tests to measure memory, sensory capacities, and other abilities. To gather his data, Dalton invented any number of machines and devices that measured human abilities and charged a small admission for members of the public to compete the tests. During this data collection period,

MOVIE - Learn about Mean and Standard Deviation

each person would complete 17 tests. He collected data from over 9000 subjects!

Associations and Mental Imagery

Galton spent some time studying the associations that we make between images and ideas that we come up with. He wrote how fascinating it was that many of the associated thoughts were from his early childhood and that he felt the unconscious had a tremendous impact on our associations. Freud would read Galton's work and was obviously very influenced by it!

Galton's study of mental imagery was one of the first applications of the questionnaire. Galton found interesting patterns in how well individuals could recall a mental image. He applied statistical analysis to the results and found that there was a normal distribution of capabilities to accurately recall details in mental images.

Animal Psychology

Since the publication of *Origin of Species* by Darwin, the notion of studying the behavior of animals as an indirect method for the study of humans began to develop. If humans are evolved from animals, then we could examine the behavior of animals, subjecting them to much more rigorous testing situations, and extrapolate the results to explain more complex human behaviors.

George John Romanes (1848-1894)

Darwin gifted his notes on animal behavior to Romanes in hopes that he would continue to study the impact of evolution on the mind as Darwin had explored its influence on the body. Romanes did not disappoint. His book, *Animal Intelligence,* is considered to be the first real text on Comparative Psychology. Romanes felt that mental capacities among animals was fundamentally akin to the mental capacities among humans, just differing in degree.

Law of Parsimony

While it was attractive to consider that animals had the same mental capacities as did humans, it was Morgan's **Law of Parsimony** that provided an alternative approach. This "law" stated, in regard to this particular question, that animal behavior must not be interpreted as the outcome of higher mental processes if it can be explained in terms of lower mental processes.

The **Law of Parsimony** has had far reaching impacts on theory building across the profession. Expanded, it promotes the idea that when looking at solutions to a question the most simple explanation is likely the correct one.

Assessment

Chapter 6 Discussion

Consider the four influences that Darwin had on the world of Psychology. Select ONE of them and reflect your thoughts on how this influence is still present today in the study of Psychology. Make an effort to include comments that are unique from your peers' comments. Select different influences if one or more has already been discussed.

Chapter 6 Quiz

1. Reflect on the Law of Parsimony and its preference for the least complex explanation. How has this "law" helped and/or hindered the pursuit of knowledge and problem solving?

Functionalism: Development and Founding

7

Attention

John Dewey on Education

John Dewey (1859-1952) had a pronounced impact on our view of Education today. Dewey always considered schools to be social institutions in which social interactions construct the elements of social reform and social change.

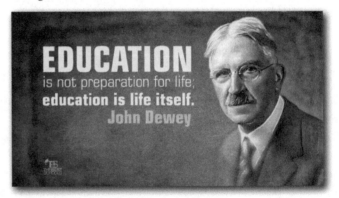

Dewey felt strongly that the purpose of schools is to allow students to interact with the curriculum and take part in their own learning. He also felt that aside from learning facts and knowledge, students should learn to think so that they can use their abilities for the greater good.

Dewey also had thoughts on the actual process of education. He felt that the most effective way to teach is to make connections between the new material and material that they already know. However, he was equally alarmed by child-centered curriculum that gave too much power to the student and undermined the role of the curriculum and the teacher.

Teaching should be a balance between delivering knowledge and taking into account the interests and experiences of the students. Dewey's work went on to influence the development of such educational concepts as experiential learning and problem-based learning.

Dewey had tremendous impact on the education of new teachers in the following ways:

1. Emphasis on the role of teachers and teaching as a social service whereas their products, students, will produce future progress.

2. A teachers should possess a passion for knowledge and an intellectual curiosity in the material and methods they teach.

3. Teachers must possess the skill to watch for and respond to the movements of the mind.

4. Teachers should conduct themselves to the upmost of social values and integrity. They are shaping the mental moral and spiritual lives of others.

Learning Outcomes

Upon completion of this Chapter, students should be able to:

1. Discuss the applications of Social Darwinism.

2. Describe the relationship between the Structural and Functional perspectives in Psychology.

Teaching

Herbert Spencer (1820-1903)

We learned a little about Herbert Spencer in the last chapter. His popularity in America was unparalleled. His coined phrase, "Survival of the Fittest" was introducing the natural order of Darwinism and Evolution to an ever increasing number of aspects of human existence. From an economic stand point, he advocated that economies be left alone and unfettered by regulations and government control. The natural forces of evolution would take over, and the "fittest" would survive, to the betterment of all.

This message fit well with the individualistic and business culture. America was founded on the principles of hard working people who believed in free enterprise, self-sufficiency, and independence from government regulations. Spencer was an intellectual "messiah" to this message and the business world in the US.

Synthetic Philosophy

Using the term "synthetic" to mean create or synthesize, Spencer's philosophy sought to apply evolutionary thought to all manner of human knowledge and experience. All things, including the mind, exist in their current form because of past and continuing efforts to adapt to changing environmental conditions.

Even machines, the inventions of people, have evolved over the years based on changing needs and environmental demands. Yesterday's machines are tossed away and become "extinct" in favor of a new "species." Samual Butler expressed to Darwin his prediction that the evolution of machines was far out-pacing that of the animals and that someday machines would achieve the full mental capacities of their creators.

William James (1842-1910)

James initiation into the world of Psychology was, interestingly, through a curiosity in the impact of mind-altering drugs. James was interested in the relationship between the mind and the body, between physiology and psychology.

The Principles of Psychology

Despite its author's eccentricity, the textbook is remarkable.

1. James writing was clear and understandable, a rarity in science.

2. He opposed Wundt's goal for psychology (the analysis of the components of consciousness.)

3. James offered an alternative view of the mind in line with Functionalism.

4. He defined the major focus point that would shape American Psychology, the study of living people and how they adapt to their environment.

5. He gave credit to the non-rational, or emotional, aspects of our lives.

James published *The Principles of Psychology* in 1890. This book remains the most influential textbook every written on Psychology. After its publication, James left the field of Psychology for good.

According to James, consciousness must be examined in its natural setting. Human events are not experienced as collections of individual parts (as Wundt would support) but we fuse these together into a cohesive whole. From this James came up with the term **Stream of Consciousness**.

The phrase "Stream of Consciousness" captures the ever-changing way in which we really experience our thoughts (at times.) According to James, our thoughts are continuous and we move from one thought to the other rather seamlessly. Since we can only pay attention to a few things at a time, we actively filter out and select specific stimuli to pay attention to. The function of this consciousness is to allow us to adapt to environmental challenges and make choices.

William James

William James Timeline by Cortland Pasquarelli

William James' textbook
Principles of Psychology defined the new field.

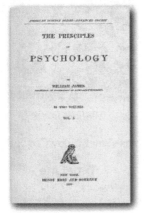

Read it Here!

Stream of consciousness.

As you can see, these ideas were really laying down the foundations for what we now know as the processes of sensation and perception. In James' writing you can also perceive the fundamental aspects of the Gestalt approach to cognition. The putting together of the parts of a situation to create a cohesive whole that has more meaning than simply the combination of the parts.

Summary of James' Contributions

1. **Pragmatism** - The validity of an idea must be demonstrated by its practical consequences. Something is valid if it works.

2. **Theory of Emotions** - James felt that emotions were first experienced as bodily reactions to a stimuli, and then we label them as specific emotions.

3. **Three Part Self** - We are made up of the material self (body, family, home, etc.), the social self (recognition from other people), and the spiritual self (our inner subjective being.)

4. **Habit** - Certain patterns of behavior, once repeated a certain number of times, become embodied in the nervous system freeing up the brain to focus on other things.

Women in Psychology

At this point in history it is still very much a challenge for women to become Psychologists. The discrimination against women in higher eduction, in general, was supported by pseudoscience conclusions about the "limited capacity" of "inferior" female brains. Two women would utilize the methods of Functional Psychology to prove the men wrong.

Helen Bradford Thompson Woolley (1874-1947) wrote her dissertation based on a functional study of the capacities of men and women on a number of psychological tests. She found that there was no difference between men and women's performance on these tests.

Leta Stetter Hollingworth's (1886-1939) research challenged the notion that the variability of women's mental functioning was limited. Her data indicated that the variability of intellectual capabilities among women are equal to the variability among men.

Granville Stanley Hall (1844-1824)

Hall's prominence in the history of Psychology is marked by how many firsts he was to be a part of. He was the first recipient of a PhD in Psychology in an American college, he established the first Psychology Lab in the US, established the first American journal in psychology, and founded (and was the first President) of the American Psychological Association.

Although he had many interests in Psychology, Hall's primary emphasis was the theory of evolution. Hall really felt that the field of Psychology should focus most of its efforts on understanding the development of children.

He proposed that the normal growth of the human mind mirrors the evolutionary stages that it has gone through in history.

G. Stanley Hall

His **Recapitulation Theory** supported that as children move through their normal stages of development, they repeat the life history of the human race...moving from a near savage state in infancy to a rational, civilized human in adulthood.

Interestingly, as Hall grew older, he began to be interested in the second half of life. He wrote the book *Senescence* about the issues of old age.

The Founding of Functionalism

Functionalism was never so much a school of thought. Its founders had no interest in founding a new, dogmatic school within the field of Psychology. They simply resisted the limits of Wundt's Experimental Psychology and Titchener's Structural approach.

Dewey, Angell, and the Chicago School

Dewey's **Reflex Arc** attempted to counter the prevailing thoughts of Wundt and Titchener by implying that behavior could not be broken down into separate parts.

He felt that the process by which a reflex occurred could not be broken down so consciousness could not be broken down either. All behavior should be seen in terms of its significance to the organism adapting to its environment.

John Dewey

Angell was the one who structured the Psychology Department at the University of Chicago, turned it into the the most influential Department, and defined Functional Psychology as a separate entity from Structural Psychology.

James Angell (1869-1949)

Defining Functional Psychology

In his textbook, Angell outlined the essentials of Functional Psychology:

The function of consciousness is to improve the organism's adaptive abilities. The goal of psychology is to study how the mind assists the organism in adjusting to its environment.

1. Functional Psychology is the psychology of mental operations (versus mental elements.)

2. Functional Psychology is the psychology of the fundamental utilities of consciousness, split between the needs of the individual and the needs of the environment.

3. Functional Psychology is the psychology of psychophysical relations and is concerned with the total relationship between the organism and its environment.

Dynamic Psychology

Robert Woodsworth introduced the concept of **motivation** into Functional Psychology. By this he emphasized the psychological events that underlie behavior. He felt that Psychology should focus on trying to understand why people do the things that they do.

We will see that motivation is a key concept that will become the focus of study in Psychology

Assessment

Chapter 7 Discussion - Darwinism

Social Darwinism applies the concept of Natural Selection and Evolution to an understanding of social structures and societies. Discuss ways in which you may value the concept of "Survival of the Fittest." In what ways do we see this is a valid and constructive philosophy?

Chapter 7 Quiz

Consider the Structural and Functional perspectives in Psychology and answer the following questions:

1. When you consider your current understanding of your own Psychology, which approach seems to make more sense to you and why?

2. Provide an analysis of a personal experience and describe it from the Structural perspective.

3. Provide an analysis of the SAME personal experience and describe it from the Functional perspective.

Applied Psychology: The Legacy of Functionalism

8

Attention

Morons, Imbeciles, Idiots, and other Scientific Words

Read the Article

When Alfred Binet (1857-1911) and Theodore Simon (1872-1961) created the first IQ test, they needed to categorize results so that others could construct interventions and expectations for persons with IQ scores well below normal.

Individuals who scored below a 70 on the IQ test were considered "mentally retarded" but there were different degrees of mental retardation.

1. **Morons** - those with an IQ between 51 and 70 - adequate learning skills to complete menial tasks and communicate.

2. **Imbeciles** - those with an IQ between 26 and 50 - unable to progress past a mental age of about six.

3. **Idiot** - those with an IQ between 0 and 25 - poor motor skills, extremely limited communication, and little response to stimulus.

You might be surprised to see that these words, now used to insult people, were actually clinical categories that were connected to IQ scores.

As much as the world of Psychology is about clearly defining concepts and creating terminology, sometimes the terms leak out into **vernacular use**, meaning that the regular population starts to use these terms and they acquire a very different meaning.

It is also interesting to note that when we encountered individuals who had profoundly low IQ scores, yet they had incredible abilities, we referred to them as **Idiot-Savant**. It is not more accurately referred to as **Savant Syndrome**. If you look this up Online you can see all kinds of examples. One famous person with Savant Syndrome is Kim Peek, who was the real-life savant and inspiration for Dustin Hoffman's portrayal of Raymond Babbitt in the movie **Rain Man**. Sadly, Kim passed away in 2009.

Kim Peek (1951-2009)

Movie - Meet Kim Peek

Down Syndrome

Prior to understanding the genetics of persons with Down Syndrome, the condition was referred to as **Mongolism**, or even **Mongoloid Idiot** (to bring in the accompanying IQ designation.) An urban legend is that this terminology came about because certain facial features of persons with Down Syndrome (round faces and eyes set wide apart) was similar to people from Mongolia.

A young girl with Down Syndrome - Image from National Library of Medicine

Deaf and Dumb

This is an interesting one. The term "Dumb" means "the inability to talk."

In American Sign Language the sign for designating a deaf person involves pointing to the ear and then pointing to the mouth...a designation of "deaf and dumb."

If an individual is born deaf, it is very difficult for them to learn how to talk because, for one, they can't hear others talk, and two, they can't hear themselves talk in order to shift their tones to accurately articulate words. When these individuals do talk it tends to be in a hollow tone with very little change in articulation. The sad thing is, when people portray a "dumb" person (meaning not intelligent) there is a tendency to mimic the voice of a deaf person.

Movie - Welcome to my world of Silence

Lunatic

This word originated from the Latin *Luna* meaning the Moon (goddess). (In French the word for the moon is *lune*).

It was thought that conditions such as insanity, madness, and epilepsy were caused by lunar cycles. In astrology, when particular conjunctions with moon were used to explain mental illness as well.

Phases of the Moon

So, do people act more erratic during a full moon? Despite this being a popular notion, there is no evidence that this is true. This thought has some ancient roots, however. In Ancient Greece and Rome, philosophers felt that the Moon would also impact the fluids in the brain as it impacts the tides.

In fact, when researchers Ivan Kelly, James Rotton, and Roger Culver reviewed over 100 of these studies back in 1991, they found none of them to show a significant relationship between the moon and human behavior. Much of the research had been poorly conducted, they found, or ignored obvious variables (one study concluded that full moons increase the incidence of car accidents, ignoring the fact that nearly all the full moon nights used for data had occurred on the weekend – when car accidents are more likely no matter what).

Does a Full Moon Really Change Human Behavior?

Learning Outcomes

Upon completion of this Chapter, students should be able to:

1. Discuss the results of personal IQ testing.

2. Discuss the use of mental testing to categorize individual differences.

Teaching

Applied Psychology

While Functional Psychology was being pursued in the classrooms and laboratories in the United States, many psychologists began to see that the skills they possessed could be readily applied in the "real world." Psychologists began to bring these skills into the world of business, advertising, schools, courthouses, and mental health clinics.

Pragmatic applications of Psychology in the US provided access to a resource that was scarce for psychologists at the time, money. In about 20 years time, America became the leading global force in Psychology. Learning from the involvement of psychologists in advertising, Psychology itself embarked on a marketing campaign to promote the field to the public. Displays were put on at the Chicago Worlds Fair and the St. Louis World Fair.

Meet me at the Fair

An article about the Psychological Exhibition at the St. Louis World Fair...not such a good job in promoting Psychology!

Read about all the exhibits and inventions that appeared at this fair!

Wireless telephones, fax machines, x-ray machine, infant incubator, personal automobile, hamburgers, hot dogs, peanut butter, iced tea, and Dr. Pepper were all introduced at the St. Louis World Fair!

Economic Factors in Applied Psychology

As much as there was growth in the number of Psychology labs that were being created around the country, this was far outpaced by the number of PhDs that were being created! These individuals, many of whom did not have an independent source of income, needed to look beyond the universities and the labs for employment.

Psychology was not held in high esteem, at least not in many colleges and universities. Unlike the natural sciences like chemistry and physics, Psychology was still not considered much of a "science." Clearly the answer to both the problems of employment and of reputation was in applying Psychology to solve real world problems.

Applied Psychology in Education

One of the initial focal points for Psychology was education. Enrollment in schools was increasing dramatically and meeting these challenges created a home for Psychology.

Mental Testing

James Cattell (1860-1944) and Francis Galton (1822-1911) collaborated in a mutual interest in individual differences. Galton was a large influence on Cattell's use of statistical analysis in conducing Psychological inquiry. (He, Cattell, was also enamored by Galton's thoughts on Eugenics and promoted the sterilization of delinquents and incentives to healthy, intelligent people to marry and have children.

James Cattell was very influential in the field of Psychology through his publication of several new journals and the establishment of the American Association of University Professors.

James Cattell

While his particular approach to mental testing was not as effective, Cattell did promote the idea that Psychology would not be considered a "real science" until it developed a foundation of experiment and measurement.

The IQ Test

Alfred Binet

Self-educated in the field of Psychology, Alfred Binet (1857-1911) would become the found of modern intelligence testing. Differing from those before him, Binet felt that the measure of abilities such as memory, attention, imagination, and comprehension would provide a much more useful measure of abilities.

By request of the French Ministry of Public Education, Binet formulated a test of mental abilities based on judgement, comprehension, and reasoning. Over time this test was refined and he introduced the concept of **Mental Age**. Mental Age entailed a record of what abilities a child of a specific age should have. For example, "What should we expect a 3-year old to be able to do?"

The test was designed to determine a child's **Mental Age**, which was then compared to their **Chronological Age**, thus creating a ratio between mental age and chronological age that we currently call the **Intelligence Quotient**, or **IQ**.

MENTAL AGE	20	X 100 = 100
CHRONOLOGICAL AGE	20	IQ

MENTAL AGE	25	X 100 = 125
CHRONOLOGICAL AGE	20	IQ

MENTAL AGE	15	X 100 = 75
CHRONOLOGICAL AGE	20	IQ

Here is how IQ tests work:

Let's say you are 20 years old. Research indicates that the **average** 20 year old would get 20 out of 25 of the questions on the test correct. If **you** take the test and you score 20 out of 25 correct, then your mental age matches your chronological age. Your IQ would be 100.

If, on the other hand, you took the test and instead you scored like the average 25 year old you would have an IQ of 125. You are 20 years old, but your intelligence is like that of a 25 year old.

If you scored like a typical 15 year old, your IQ would be 75. You are 20 years old, but your intelligence is like a 15 year old.

It is important to remember, though beyond the scope of this class, that the mental abilities that are measured in an IQ test are specific to those that have been found to be correlated with success in school. They are not the only measures for intelligence, nor is school the only place where people can be successful.

Keeping in pace with the thought of Functional and Applied Psychology, the IQ test was **USEFUL** in determining who might do well in school and who might need extra help.

Learn about and take the Stanford-Binet Scale

Binet's work crossed the Atlantic by way of Henry Goddard (1866-1957) at the University of Southern California and it was published as the Binet Simon Measuring Scale for Intelligence. Lewis Terman (1877-1956) later adapted the test though his work at Stanford University and the Stanford-Binet Intelligence Scale is still with us today.

Lewis Terman Timeline by Erin Bailey

TimeLine

Lewis Terman

Applied Testing

WWI brought demands from the government to create tests that could be administered quickly and determine the intelligence of new recruits. The **Army Alpha** and **Army Beta** tests did not see implementation until the end of the war, but Psychology had responded to demands and had delivered. Millions of people subjected themselves to being tested for mental abilities and the

faith in the field of Psychology increased among the public and the government alike.

Many psychologists at this time mad a living developing and administering psychological tests.

Psychological Testing Enters a Dark Period

Cover of the controversial book, The Bell Curve, which reignited the debate on racial differences in intelligence in 1994

When we consider these early years of psychological testing and how they were applied, there was no real understanding of the impact that culture and language would have on a person's ability to score on a test. The standards for scoring were based on specific populations of people and are really only valid when measuring the abilities of those populations.

The application of Psychological Testing to screen immigrants at Ellis Island is one of these dark times in Psychology. This was further exemplified in the release of data from the WWI testing era that indicated that Blacks and those with Mediterranean or Latin American backgrounds scored lower that whites on the tests. The thought that this may be due to language barriers or cultural differences did not seem to hold.

Modern tests are constructed in a manner that takes into account this diversity. The standards by which scores are examined are also determined through a much large sample of different people from a greater diversity of cultural backgrounds.

Women in the Field of Psychology

Women continued to struggle for acceptance into the world of Psychology. The book points out a number of stories of individuals who encountered prejudice and barriers in their work simply due to sex. As with some other areas of social life, women persisted in forcing themselves into the field and made significant contributions to the work. They were also very involved in the beginnings of the Applied Psychology movement because this was, at first, considered to be beneath the level of the true scientist. Areas such as counseling were considered "woman's work"...and it became so. Almost 50% of the jobs in education and clinical settings were held by women.

Clinical Psychology

Although his practice of Clinical Psychology (more like School Psychology) is vastly different than what we see today, **Lightner Witmer** (18671956) pioneered the concept of Clinical Psychology. Witmer's life work would focus on the development of interventions to treat children.

Clinics for Child Evaluation

Witmer's clinics had no standards to apply, so they made them up. The developed tests and procedures to evaluate children's problems. Prophetically, Witmer advocated that families should also be involved in the treatment supporting his notion that if the school AND family was improved, the child's behavior would improve.

The Profession of Clinical Psychology

Early in the 1900's, the profession of Psychology was moving steadily toward advances in the treatment of mental disorders. Child clinics were set up in order to address mental health problems before they developed into more serious conditions in adulthood.

Freud entered the scene and began the transformation of Clinical Psychology, but the movement was still pretty slow in the US. It was not until WWII that the need for Clinical Psychologists grew in response to both recruits and veterans exhibiting anxiety, depression, anger, and other unstable mental conditions. As our book outlines, 1 million men were rejected for military service due to psychiatric issues, of those that were accepted, 1 million were hospitalized for psychiatric conditions while on active duty and 500,000 of these were discharged because of these conditions.

After the war, the VA (Veterans Administration) found itself responsible for over 40,000 vets diagnosed with psychiatric problems and over 3 million who needed psychological, counseling, vocational, and/or case management services. Interestingly, the VA remains the largest employer of psychologists. Today, Clinical Psychology is the most common PhD in Psychology.

APA Division 19 - Society for Military Psychology

Industrial-Organizational Psychology

Another emerging area of Applied Psychology was in the work place. These applications of Psychology to industry focused on such areas as advertising, workplace conditions, hiring practices, management, and productivity.

Advertising

Although we will see further advances in the field of advertising as a result of behavioral psychology, Scott advanced the notion that consumers do not always think rationally and they can be swayed by different messages. Using his concept of suggestibility, Scott encouraged companies to utilize specific techniques to attract customers that are still used today to:

1. Direct commands - "Buy our Product"

2. Return coupons (thanks to Scott we have coupons!!!)

3. Eliciting emotional responses to the product.

Employee Selection

Scott developed tests that could be given to groups of candidates for positions that measured such abilities as intelligence, applications of intelligence, judgement, accuracy, demeanor, sincerity, productivity, character and cognitive speed.

Walter Dill Scott (1869-1955)

Scott advanced many areas of IO Psychology and was the first person to hold the title of Professor of Applied Psychology

The Hawthorn Studies

Into the 1920s the focus of Industrial Psychology was selection and job placement. This focus was widely expanded by the studies that took place at the Hawthorn Plant of the Western Electric Company.

This study examined work conditions (lighting and temperature), human relations, motivation, and morale.

One of the important outcomes of the Hawthorn Studies actually acquired a name, the **Hawthorn Effect**. This phenomena describes the fact that when employees are questioned about their work environment by management, they very act of being involved in the process, of being observed, and being part of an effort to improve conditions, actually improves worker efficiency, productivity, and morale. Even when no effective changes have been made.

The fact is, looking back on the original study, the effect was not real and did not happen. So in the original study the "Hawthorn Effect" is a myth. However, today when we talk about the impact of the "observer" on people's performance, we elicit the term Hawthorn Effect.

Interesting things did come out of the Hawthorn Studies themselves, however, including the impact of lighting on productivity. Factories to this day usually employ unusually bright lighting in work areas in order to keep workers alert and productive and to reduce accidents.

Emerging areas in Psychology

Our book introduces us to Hugo Munsterberg (1863-1916). Despite being a controversial figure in the world of Psychology, his research into a variety of areas of applied psychology and his ability to wrote hundreds of articles and books for public consumption introduced new areas into the field of Applied Psychology. He wrote on such diverse topics as courtroom trials, the criminal justice system, advertising, vocational counseling, mental health, psychotherapy, and even the psychology of motion pictures. He is considered to have founded the field of **Forensic Psychology**.

These are areas of study that would continue to develop through the history of Psychology.

A little bit of extra stuff...

Here is some option reading for you in regard to the application of Psychology to Advertising.

The Psychology of Advertising

Below is a full article by Walter D. Scott on the Psychology of Adversing that was published in the Atlantic in 1904. The insights into the application of Psychology to advertising and influencing consumer behavior is as true today as it was then!

"Advertisements are sometimes spoken of as the nervous system of the business world ... As our nervous system is constructed to give us all the possible sensations from objects, so the advertisement which is comparable to the nervous system must awaken in the reader as many different kinds of images as the object itself can excite" Walter D. Scott, January 1904 Issue

To keep a slender figure
No one can deny...

Reach for a **LUCKY** *instead of a sweet*

LUCKY STRIKE CIGARETTES

"It's toasted"

[This article, the first of a series of studies of Modern Advertising, has been written by Walter D. Scott, Assistant Professor of Psychology in Northwestern University.—THE EDITORS.]

The only method of advertising known to the ancients was the word of mouth. The merchant who had wares to offer brought them to the gate of a city and there cried aloud, making the worth of his goods known to those who were entering the city, and who might be induced to turn aside and purchase them. We are not more amused by the simplicity of the ancients than we are amazed at the magnitude of the modern systems of advertising. From the day when Boaz took his stand by the gate to advertise Naomi's parcel of land by crying, "Ho, ... turn aside," to the day when Barnum billed the towns for his three-ringed circus, the evolution in advertising had been gradual, but it had been as great as that from the anthropoid ape to P. T. Barnum himself.

As soon as printed symbols were invented the advertising man made use of them to give publicity to his merchandise. We find advertisements engraved on walls and tombs, written on parchment and papyrus, and printed by the first printing presses. Although these various forms of advertising were employed, but little thought and care seem to have been expended upon them. Postells, painted signs, street-car placards, booklets, calendars, almanacs, handbills, magazine and newspaper advertising have now become forms of advertising so well established that we look upon them as a necessity, and are surprised to learn that most of them are modern innovations.

The first advertisement printed in English appeared in the Imperial Intelligencer in March, 1648. Advertising in magazines was not begun until comparatively recent times. For instance, the first advertisement appeared in Harper's Magazine in 1864. In this magazine more space has been devoted to advertising during the past year than the sum total of space for the twenty-four years from 1864 to 1887, inclusive. Indeed, advertising may be said to have been in its swaddling clothes until about the year 1887. The most rapid development has taken place during the last fifteen years. The change has been so great that the leading advertisers say that in comparison with to-day there was in existence fifteen years ago no advertising worthy of the name.

The gain in the quantity of advertising can be seen by observing the increase in the number of pages devoted to advertisements in any of our publications. The month of October is regarded as the typical month, therefore we present the number of pages devoted to advertisements for the month of October in Harper's Magazine for each year from the first appearance of advertisements in that magazine to the present time,— 1864, 3 ¼; '65. 2; '66, 3 ; '67, 6; '68, 7 1/3; '69, 5 1/3; '70, 4 ½; '71, 3 ½; '72, 2; '73, 1; '74. 0; '75, 0; '76, 0; '77, 0; '78, 0; '79, 0; '80, 0; '81, 0; '82, 1 ¼; '83, 8 ½; '84, 8; '85, 11 ½; '86, 20; '87, 37; '88, 54; '89, 48: '90, 73; '91 80 ½; '92, 87; '93, 77 ½; '94, 75 ¾; '95, 78 ¼; '96, 73; '97, 80 ¾; '98, 81 ¾; '99, 106 ¾; 1900, 97 ½; '01, 93 ½; '02, 128; '03, 141.

It will be noticed in the data as given above that during the years of special prosperity there was a very great increase in the volume of advertising while there was but a slight falling off following a financial depression. The increase was not pronounced until about 1887, but from that time on it has been very marked, not only in Harper's, but in almost all of our publications.

There has not only been an increase in the number of advertising pages in the individual publications, but the number of publications has increased enormously of recent years. The increase of population in the United States has been rapid during the last fifty years, but the increase in the total number of copies of the different publications has been many fold greater. Thus the distribution of the copies of these periodicals to each individual was as follows:— In 1850 each individual received on the average 18 copies from one or more of these periodicals: in 1860, 29; in 1870, 39; in 1880, 41; in 1890, 74; in 1900, 107.

A significant cause of this increase is the reduction in the subscription price which is made possible because of the profit accruing to such publications from their advertisements. The total income secured from subscriptions for all these publications last year was less than the amount paid for the advertising pages. We have this current year about 20,000 periodicals carrying advertisements, each with a constantly increasing number of pages devoted to them, and with a rapidly advancing rate secured for each advertisement. In addition to this, the increase is phenomenal in the use of booklets, posters. painted signs, street-car placards, almanacs, and many other forms of advertising. One firm is supposed to have distributed 25,000,000 almanacs in a single year.

The expense connected with these various forms of printed advertising reaches far into the millions. One authority puts the total annual expense of printed forms of advertising at six hundred million dollars. This sum does not seem to be an exaggeration. Mr. Post spends as much as six hundred thousand dollars annually in advertising his food products. One million dollars was spent last year in advertising Force. Over six hundred thousand dollars is spent annually in advertising Ayer's remedies; and over one million dollars in advertising Peruna.

The advertising rate has been advanced repeatedly in many magazines during the last few years. Firms which formerly paid but one hundred dollars for a full-page advertisement in the Century Magazine now pay two hundred and fifty dollars for the same amount of space. The Ladies' Home Journal has increased its advertising rate to six dollars for a single agate line (there are fourteen agate lines to the inch), the width of one column, for a single insertion. The cost of a full page for a single issue is four thousand dollars. The Procter & Gamble Co. have made a three years' contract for a single page in each issue, to he devoted to the advertisement of Ivory Soap. For this space they pay four thousand dollars a mouth, forty-eight thousand dollars a year, and one hundred and forty-four thousand dollars for the term of three years. Think of the risk a firm runs in investing four thousand dollars in a single page advertisement! How can they expect to get back the equivalent of such a sum of money from a single advertisement?

There are very many advertisements that do not pay. One man has roughly estimated that seventy-five per cent of all advertisements do not pay; yet the other twenty-five per cent pay so well that there is scarcely a business man who is willing to stand idly by and allow his competitors to do the advertising. The expense connected with advertising has increased; the competition between rival firms has become keener; and consequently the demand for good advertising has become imperative. The number of unsuccessful advertisements are many, and yet the loss incurred in an unsuccessful advertising campaign is so great that many firms stand aghast at the thought of such an undertaking. Many merchants see the necessity of advertising their business, but feel unable to enter the arena and compete with successful rivals.

The day of reckless, sporadic, haphazard advertising is rapidly coming to an end so far as magazine advertising is concerned. Although the number of pages devoted to advertising in our best magazines has increased during the last ten years, the number of firms advertising in these same magazines has decreased. The struggle has been too fierce for any but the strongest. The inefficient advertisers are gradually being eliminated, and the survival of the fittest seems to be a law of advertising as it is of everything else that develops.

The leaders of the profession feel that their work has grown till it is beyond their control and comprehension. They have been successful, and hardly know how it has all come about. The men who have been the most successful are often the ones who feel most deeply their inability to meet new emergencies. They believe that there should be some underlying principles which could help them in analyzing what they have already accomplished, and assist them in their further efforts. As their entire object is to produce certain effects on the minds of possible customers, it is not strange that they have turned to psychology in search of such principles. Traditionally the practical business man scouts at theory. Psychology, to the popular mind, is something devoid of all practical application, related to metaphysics, and suited only to the recluse and the hermit. If ever there was ground to expect sarcastic and pessimistic prophecies from the hardheaded business man, it was when it was proposed to establish advertising on a theoretical basis deduced from psychology. Such adverse criticism has, however, been the exception. The American business man is not afraid of theories. He wants them, and the more the better.

The best thought of the advertising world finds expression in the advertising journals and in the addresses delivered by various experts at gatherings of professional advertisers. In 1895 in one of the leading advertising journals appeared the following editorial: "Probably when we are a little more enlightened, the advertisement writer, like the teacher, will study psychology. For, however diverse their occupations may at first sight appear, the advertisement writer and the teacher have one great object in common—to influence the human mind. The teacher has a scientific foundation for his work in that direction, but the advertisement writer is really also a psychologist. Human nature is a great factor in advertising success; and he who writes advertisements without reference to it is apt to find that he has reckoned without his host." The man who penned this editorial was a practical advertiser, but he admitted of no incongruity between the practical and the theoretical.

In Publicity, for March, 1901, appeared a leading article on psychology and advertising. The following is a quotation from it:—

"The time is not far away when the advertising writer will find out the inestimable benefits of a knowledge of psychology. The preparation of copy has usually followed the instincts rather than the analytical functions. An advertisement has been written to describe the articles which it was wished to place before the reader; a bit of cleverness, an attractive cut, or some other catchy device has been used, with the hope that the hit or miss ratio could be made as favorable as possible. But the future must needs be full of better methods than these to make advertising advance with the same rapidity as it has during the latter part of the last century. And this will come through a closer knowledge of the psychological composition of the mind. The so-called 'students of human nature' will then be called successful psychologists, and the successful advertisers will be likewise termed psychological advertisers. The mere mention of psychological terms, habit, self, conception, discrimination, association, memory, imagination and perception, reason, emotion, instinct and will, should create a flood of new thought that should appeal to every advanced consumer of advertising space."

In in address before the Agate Club of Chicago the speaker said: "As advertisers, all your efforts have been to produce certain effects on the minds of possible customers. Psychology is, broadly speaking, the science of the mind. Art is the doing and science is the understanding how to do, or the explanation of what has been done. If we are able to find and to express the psychological laws upon which the art of advertising is based, we shall have made a distinct advance, for we shall have added the science to the art of advertising."

In a recent address before the Atlas Club of Chicago the speaker said: "In passing to the psychological aspect of our subject, advertising might properly be defined as the art of determining the will of possible customers. . . . Our acts are the resultants of our motives, and it is your function in commercial life to create the motives that will effect the sale of the producer's wares."

In response to this felt need on the part of the advertiser, several students of psychology have tried to select those principles of psychology which might be of benefit to the advertiser, and to present them to the advertising world through pamphlets,1 magazine articles,2 public addresses,3 and, in one case at least, by means of a book.4

The method employed by the psychologist in attempting to give advertising a theoretical basis has been quite uniform. He has first analyzed the human mind into its various activities, then analyzed advertisements to discover what there is in them that may or may not awaken the activity desired. This method can best be understood from an example. For an illustration we shall consider Mental Imagery as understood by the psychologist and in its application to advertising.

The man who is born blind is not only unable to see objects, but he is equally unable to imagine how they look. After we have looked at objects we can see them in our mind's eye with more or less distinctness, even if our eyes are closed or the object is far removed from us. When we imagine how an absent object looks we are said to have a visual image of it. We cannot imagine how a thing looks unless we have actually seen it in our previous experience. The imagination can take the data of former experience and unite them into new forms, but all the details of the new formation must be taken from the former experience of the individual.

The man who is born deaf can neither hear nor imagine what sounds are like. Whatever we have heard, we can live over again in imagination,—we can form auditory images of it. We cannot imagine any sound which we have not actually heard, although we can unite into new combinations the sounds and tones which we have experienced.

I can imagine how beefsteak tastes, but I cannot imagine the taste of hashish, for in all my past experience I never have tasted it, and do not even know which one of my former experiences it is like. If I knew that it tasted like pepper, or like pepper and vinegar mixed, I could form some sort of an image of its taste; but as it is I am perfectly helpless when I try to imagine it. I can, with more or less success, imagine how everything tastes which I have eaten, but I cannot imagine the taste of a thing which I have not touched to my tongue. Analogous descriptions could be given of images of movements, of smell, of touch, of heat, of cold, of pressure, and of pain.

We have no direct knowledge of the minds of our neighbors; we assume that their thinking is very much like ours, for their actions—outward expressions of thought—are so similar to ours. It was formerly assumed that, given any particular object of thought, all normal minds would reach the same conclusion concerning it, and, furthermore, the different stages in the line of thought and the "mind stuff" would be the same throughout. Such a conception is wholly false. Normal minds reach different conclusions under apparently identical outward circumstances, but there is a greater difference in the terms of thought, or the mind stuff with which the thinking is done. One man thinks in terms of sight. He is said to be "eye-minded." His thinking is a rapid succession of pictures. When he thinks of a violin he thinks rather how it looks than how it sounds.

Another man thinks in terms of sound. He is "ear-minded." His thinking is a succession of sounds. When he thinks of his friends he hears their voices, but cannot possibly imagine how they look. He does not know that there are other possible forms of thought, and so assumes that all people think in terms of sound as he does. If he should describe a battle his description would be full of the roar and tumult of the strife. Another man is "motor-minded." He thinks in terms of movements. Even when he looks at a painting he whispers inaudibly to himself a description of the painting. Later when he describes the picture to a friend he may do it in the terms which he whispered to himself when he was looking at the picture.

Thus it has been found that there are great personal differences in normal individuals in their ability to form certain classes of mental images.

All persons seem to be able to form at least unclear and indistinct visual images; most persons seem to have some ability in forming auditory images; very many can imagine movements with some degree of satisfaction. There are many who cannot imagine how pickles taste; others cannot imagine the odor of a flower. There are persons who have a limited ability to form all sorts of images, but most persons have a very decided ability for one class and a corresponding weakness for others. This difference in the ease with which certain classes of images can be formed, as well as the difference in individuals in imagining different classes of sensations, is followed with practical consequences.

In a former age the seller, the buyer, and the commodity were brought together. The seller described and exhibited his wares. The buyer saw the goods, heard of them, tasted them, smelt them, felt, and lifted them. He tested them by means of every sense organ to which they could appeal. In this way the buyer became acquainted with the goods. His perception of them was as complete as it could be made. In these latter days the market-place has given way to the office. The consequent separation of buyer, seller, and commodity made the commercial traveler with his sample case seem a necessity. But, with the glowing volume of business, and with the increased need for more economical forms of transacting business, the printed page, as a form of advertisement, has superseded the market-place, and is, in many cases, displacing the commercial traveler. In this transition from the market-place and the commercial traveler to the printed page, the advertiser must be on his guard to preserve as many as possible of the good features of the older institutions. In the two older forms of barter all the senses of the purchaser were appealed to, if possible, and in addition to this the word of mouth of the seller was added to increase the impressions, and to call special attention to the strong features of the commodity. In the printed page the word of mouth is the only feature which is of necessity entirely absent. Indeed, the printed page cannot appeal directly to any of the senses except the eye, but the argument may be of such a nature that the reader's senses are appealed to indirectly through his imagination.

The function of our nervous system is to make us aware of the sights, sounds, feelings, tastes, etc, of the objects in our environment, and the more sensations we receive from an object the better we know it. The nervous system which does not respond to sound or to any other of the sensible qualities is a defective nervous system. Advertisements are sometimes spoken of as the nervous system of the business world. That advertisement of musical instruments which contains nothing to awaken images of sound is a defective advertisement. That advertisement of foods which contains nothing to awaken images of taste is a defective advertisement. As our nervous system is constructed to give us all the possible sensations from objects, so the advertisement which is comparable to the nervous system must awaken in the reader as many different kinds of images as the object itself can excite.

A person can he appealed to most easily and most effectively through his dominating imagery. Thus one who has visual images that are very clear and distinct appreciates descriptions of scenes. The one who has strong auditory imagery delights in having auditory images awakened. It is in general best to awaken as many different classes of images as possible, for in this way variety is given, and each reader is appealed to in the sort of imagery which is the most pleasing to him, in which he thinks most readily, and by means of which he is most easily influenced.

One of the great weaknesses of the present day advertising is found in the fact that the writer of the advertisement fails to appeal thus indirectly to the senses. How many advertisers describe a piano so vividly that the reader can hear it? How many food products are so described that the reader can taste the food? How many advertisements describe a perfume so that the reader can smell it? How many describe an undergarment so that the reader can feel the pleasant contact with his body? Many advertisers seem never to have thought of this, and make no attempt at such descriptions.

The cause of this deficiency is twofold. In the first place, it is not easy in type to appeal to any other sense than that of sight. Other than visual images are difficult to awaken when the means employed is the printed page. In the second place, the individual writers are deficient in certain forms of mental imagery, and therefore are not adepts in describing articles in terms which to themselves are not significant. This second ground for failure in writing effective advertisements will be made clear by the examples taken from current advertisements which are quoted below.

A piano is primarily not a thing to look at or an object for profitable investment, but it is a musical instrument. It might be beautiful and cheap, but still be very undesirable. The chief thing about a piano is the quality of its tone. Many advertisers of pianos do not seem to have the slightest appreciation of this fact.

When they attempt to describe a piano they seem as men groping in the dark. Their statements are general and meaningless. As an example of such a failure the advertisement of the Knabe Piano is typical:—

The KNABE

Its successful growth and experience of nearly seventy years guarantees to new friends the greatest degree to tried and tested excellence, judged from any standpoint of criticism or comparison.

WM. KNABE & CO.

NEW YORK BALTIMORE WASHINGTON

This is a half-page advertisement, but it contains no illustration, makes no reference to tone or to any other quality of music, and does not even suggest that the Knabe is a musical instrument at all. Many advertisers describe the appearance and durability of the case or the cost of the entire instrument, but ordinarily their statements are so general that the advertisement could be applied equally well to perfumes, fountain pens, bicycles, automobiles, snuff, or sausages, but would be equally inefficient if used to advertise any of them. They do not describe or refer in any way to the essential characteristics of a piano. They awaken no images of sound; they do not make us hear a piano in our imagination.

The following is a quotation in full of an advertisement of the Vose Piano, but with the words "sewing machine" substituted for "piano." This advertisement, like the one quoted above, contains no illustration, and it will be noted that there is nothing in the text which does not apply equally well to a sewing machine.

Many of the advertisements of the Emerson, Weber, Everett, and of a few other piano firms are equally poor attempts to present the desirable features of pianos.

In recent advertisements of the Blasius piano an attempt is made to present a piano as a musical instrument. A music score is used as the background of the advertisement; there is a cut of a young lady playing the piano; and in the text appear these expressions: "Excellent tone," "the sweetest tone I ever heard," "sweet and melodious in tone," "like a grand church organ for power and volume: and a brilliant, sweet-tuned piano in one." Thus the background, the illustration, and the text all unite to awaken images of sound, and to suggest that about a piano which is the real ground for desiring such an instrument.

In determining which foods I shall eat it is a matter of some importance to know how the goods are manufactured, what the prices are, how they are prepared for the table, and whether they are nourishing or harmful to my system. The one essential element, however, is the taste. When I look over a bill of fare I choose what I think will taste good. When I order groceries I order what pleases and tickles my palate. I want the food that makes me smack my lips, that makes my mouth water. Under these circumstances all other considerations are minimized to the extreme.

In advertisements of food products it is surprising to note that many foods are advertised as if they had no taste at all. One would suppose that the food was to be taken by means of a hypodermic injection, and not by the ordinary process of taking the food into the mouth and hence into contact with the organ of taste. The advertisers seem to be at a loss to know what to say about their foods, and so have, in many cases, expressed themselves in such general terms that their advertisements could be applied to any product whatever.

The following is the complete text of a full-page advertisement which appeared in recent magazines. The only change is that here we have substituted "scouring soap" for the name of the commodity:

"The grocer's smile. The smile that won't come off.
More scouring soap the grocer said,
No other brand will do instead;
And o'er his kindly features spread
The smile that won't come off.
Look for the coupon in the package."

The illustration was that of a grocer looking at a package which might as well have been scouring soap as Quaker Oats. There is nothing to suggest taste.

Some advertisers of food are evidently chronic dyspeptics, and take it for granted that all others are in the same condition. They have nothing to say about their foods except that they have wonderful medicinal properties. To me a food which is only healthful savors of hospitals and sickrooms, and is something which a well man would not want.

There are other advertisers who appreciate the epicurean tendency of the ordinary man and woman. They describe food in such a way that we immediately want what they describe. The man who wrote the following advertisement belongs to this class:

"That very old proverb about reaching the heart of a man is best exemplified with Nabisco sugar wafers. A fairy sandwich with an upper and a lower crust of indescribable delicacy, separated with a creamy flavor of lemon, orange, chocolate, vanilla, strawberry, raspberry, or mint. Ask for your favorite flavor."

The picture represents a beautiful young lady presenting a gentleman with the commodity described.

This advertisement has character and individuality. Its statements could not be applied to anything but foods, and, indeed, to nothing but Nabisco. They do not say that Nabisco is healthy, but when I read them I feel sure that Nabisco would agree with me.

This illustration of the way in which one chapter of psychology (Mental Imagery) can be applied to advertising is but one of a score of illustrations which could be given. Psychology has come to be one of the most fascinating of all the sciences, and bids fair to become of as great practical benefit as physics and chemistry. As these latter form the theoretical basis for all forms of industry which have to do with matter, so psychology must form the theoretical basis for all forms of endeavor which deal with mind.

The householder in glancing through his morning paper has his attention caught by the more attractive advertisements. The mechanic in going to and from his place of employment whiles away his time in looking at the display cards in the trolley or the elevated cars. The business man can scarcely pass a day without being forced to look at the advertisements which stare at him from the bill boards. The members of the family turn over the advertising pages in their favorite magazine, not because they are forced to, but because they find the advertisements so interesting and instructive. These persons are oblivious to the enormous expense which the merchant has incurred in securing these results. They are unconscious of the fact that the results secured are the ones sought for, and that in planning the advertising campaign the merchant has made a study of the minds of these same householders, mechanics, business men, and members of the family. Advertising is an essential factor in modern business methods, and to advertise wisely the business man must understand the workings of the minds of his customers, and must know how to influence them effectively,—he must know how to apply psychology to advertising.

On the Psychology of Advertising. Professor HARLOW GALE, author and publisher: Minneapolis, Minn. 1900.

Mahin's Magazine, Chicago. This magazine contains monthly articles on The Psychology of Advertising.

Found in the published proceedings of the various advertising clubs.

The Theory of Advertising. By WALTER DILL SCOTT. Boston: Small, Maynard & Co. 1903.

Assessment

Chapter 8 Discussion A - Intelligence

Using the link to the Stanford-Binet Scale, take this intelligence test. Report out your results and reflect on what the test actually tells you about your intelligence. In your opinion, are intelligence tests biased against members of minority groups? Defend your answer.

The Stanford-Binet Scale and Test

Chapter 8 Discussion B - Decisions

Reflect on the methods of mental testing and their applications. We use tests to measure intelligence, to place people in courses, to apply for college, to get jobs, to get a diagnosis, etc. Key decisions in our lives are made in consult with the answers we provide on tests. What are the advantages and limits of this kind of testing?

Behaviorism: Antecedent Influences

9

Attention

Pavlov's Dogs and the Nazi Siege on Stalingrad

Pavlov's work with his dogs occurred in the 1890s. Pavlov himself died on February 27, 1936. His dogs lived on in the institute in which he did his work. The institute was located in the city Stalingrad (now St. Petersburg) and was a target of the Nazi invasion of Russia during WWII.

Ivan Pavlov and his Associates in his Lab in Stalingrad

There is probably no more well known siege than the one on Stalingrad by the German army. The German's surrounded the city on September 2nd 1941 with the intent of starving the entire citizenry and then utterly destroying the city. The siege did not lift until January 27th, 1944. 872 days without food, water, medical care, etc.

In that time it is estimated that 1,500,000 soldiers and civilians died. People were starving to death, and dropping in the streets. As the siege wore on, all the pet stores, zoos, and any animal menagerie were raided for food. The poor dogs of Pavlov's lab were no exception.

The staff and locals of the lab ate the dogs in an attempt to survive the Nazi siege.

Learning Outcomes

Upon completion of this Chapter, students should be able to:

1. Discuss the notion of animal behavior being analogous to human behavior.

2. Apply the concepts of Classical Conditioning to the analysis of a print advertisement.

Teaching

The Problem is...Introspection

John B. Watson

Leading into the early 1910s and 1920s, the problem with Psychology, according to **John B. Watson** (1878-1958), was the rather unscientific process of introspection. Watson declared that the science of Psychology should instead focus its efforts on what is directly observable and measurable. All else is simply speculation as to what is happening in the mind. He recognized that there needed to be an increased objectivity in the field of Psychology.

Animal Psychology and Behaviorism

Darwin's contribution to science, evolution, had an amazing impact on the study of Psychology. One such impact was Comparative Psychology. This field promoted the idea that if all humans are descendant from more simple animals, then we can study simple animals and make inferences about humans.

Early researchers developed notions that all aspects of the human experience with present in lower animals (and even plants.) Motivated behavior and discriminate perception were attributed to micro-organisms and even plants were thought to have a degree of consciousness.

What we see at this time is a sort-of return to the **automaton** perspective of animals. Rejecting the anthropomorphic (seeing human-characteristics in animals and plants) viewpoint, scientists began to see animal behavior as simply a "response" to a "stimulus." Keeping with the aforementioned **parsimony** approach, this simpler view of animal behavior better explained observations. Consciousness was not the same in animals, memory itself was a set of learned **associations** between specific stimuli and responses.

The Relation of Strength of Stimulus to Rapidity of Habit Formation

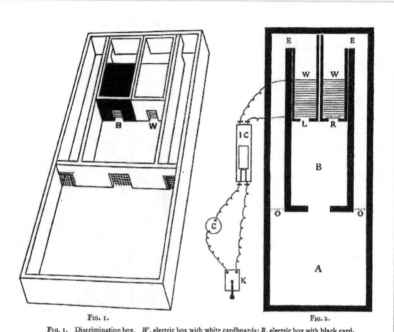

FIG. 1.

FIG. 2.

FIG. 1. Discrimination box. *W*, electric box with white cardboards; *B*, electric box with black cardboards.

FIG. 2. Ground plan of discrimination box. *A*, nest-box; *B*, entrance chamber; *W W*, electric boxes; *L*, doorway of left electric box; *R*, doorway of right electric box; *E*, exit from electric box to alley; *O*, swinging door between alley and *A*; *IC*, induction apparatus; *C*, electric battery; *K*, key in circuit.

An example of a maze for analyzing the behavior of rats.

This early work with animals and the movement toward a more objective focus of the field of Psychology set the stage for a new movement.

The First Behaviorists

Edward Lee Thorndike (1874-1949)

Thorndike agreed that the focus of Psychological study should be on objectively, observable behavior.

Thorndike worked with animals to get himself into the world of Psychology but he quickly began to work with humans. He was a prolific writer and established the Journal of Educational Psychology.

Thorndike's concept of **connectionism** is a build on the term **association** (and the term association is the one that has lasted the test of time.) Thorndike created any number of puzzle boxes that posed challenges to his animals. They had to learn how to unlatch the box to get out. As the animal learned the process to get out, he would record the number of wrong attempts and the amount of attempts it took for the animal to learn the puzzle.

Edward Thorndike

I believe that Thorndike would have been absolutely thrilled with the notion of todays "Escape Rooms" for people! This is nothing more than a human-level "puzzle box" where the people in the room need to solve puzzles and find clues in order to escape from the room.

Check out Mainly Escapes

The Only Laws in Psychology

Many of the sciences have many "laws" that govern the ways in which the world works. In physics we have the Law of Gravity, the Law of Thermodynamics, and the Law of Conservation of Energy...just to name a few.

There are not many parallels in the relatively more gray areas of Psychology. Thorndike came up with two!

1. **The Law of Effect** - presenting these ideas as "stamping in" and "stamping out" (later to referred to as "reinforcement" and "punishment") the Law of Effect states that any behavior that is followed by a satisfying consequence or stimulus will be more likely to occur again. Likewise, and behavior that is followed by an unsatisfactory or uncomfortable consequence or stimulus will occur less often, and may not occur at all.

2. **The Law of Exercise** - this law suggests that the more times a particular behavior is associated with the resulting consequences the more strongly the two become associated.

Ivan Pavlov (1849-1936)

Pavlov contributed immensely to three areas of interest.

1. The functions of the nerves of the heart.

2. Primary digestive glands (for which he earned the 1904 Nobel Prize)

3. Conditioned reflexes (which is his contribution to Psychology)

Pavlov observed that if he placed a piece of bread in a dog's mouth the dog would salivate. He felt that this was not a learned process and termed it an **unconditioned reflex**. The sight of the bread, however, which would also elicit salivation, had to be learned, which he termed a **conditioned stimulus**.

Pavlov and his assistants experimented with all sorts of stimuli to "associate" or "condition" the response of salivation, and his classic experiment with the bell was born.

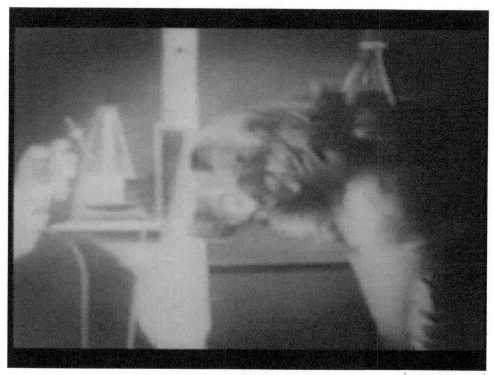

MOVIE - Classical Conditioning

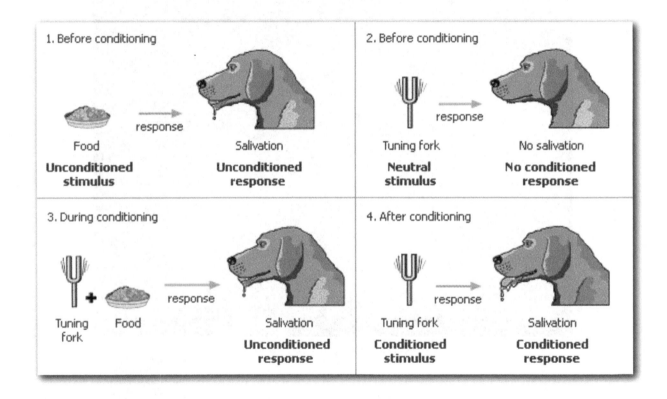

Assessment

Chapter 9 Discussion - Animals

The work with animals, deeply connected to the concept of evolution, supposes that by studying animals we can better understand humans. Discuss how you feel about this. Can studying animals really give us insight into human behavior?

Chapter 9 Assignment - Behavior

Purpose

The purpose of this assignment is to provide you the opportunity to apply the concepts of Classical Conditioning as put forth by Pavlov. The most current use of Classical Conditioning is in the field of advertising where images and emotions are paired with products in order to influence buying behavior.

Understanding the underlying psychology of advertising allows one to appreciate the powerful influence the media has on attitudes and behavior.

Skills and Knowledge

You will demonstrate the following skills and knowledge by completing this assignment:

1. Defining terms related to Classical Conditioning including unconditioned stimulus, unconditioned response, conditioned stimulus, conditioned response, and neutral stimulus.

2. Apply an understanding of Classical Conditioning to the analysis of a print advertisement.

3. Write a title page and paper in a word processor.

4. Pasting an image into a digital document.

5. Upload the paper to the assignment drop box.

Task

For this assignment you are going to find a print-based (or web-based image) of an advertisement. You will need to secure a digital copy of the ad to include in your submission.

After your title page, place the image at the top of your first page. Below, in outline format, identify the components of the advertisement, including:

1. Unconditioned Stimulus

2. Unconditioned Response

3. Neutral Stimulus

4. Conditioned Stimulus

5. Conditioned Response

When you have completed this part of the assignment, write a brief statement describing the characteristics of the "audience" this advertisement was meant to attract. Support your answers.

Criteria for Success

Use the rubric below as a guide to this assignment.

Title Page   10 points

Standard title page with name, date, course, college name and the name of the assignment.

Image of Advertisement   20 points

The ad is pasted into the document.

Unconditioned Stimulus   10 points

Correctly identified the US.

Unconditioned Response   10 points

Correctly identified the UC.

Neutral Stimulus   10 points

Correctly identified the NS.

Conditioned Stimulus   10 points

Correctly identified the CS.

Conditioned Response   10 points

Correctly identified the CR.

Essay on Audience   10 points

Sound logic and rational for audience choice.

Mechanics   10 points

Spelling, syntax, and organizational structure of the paper. Clear and organized.

Behaviorism: The Beginnings

10

Attention

Popular Psychology

Psychology is a popular subject. As you will see in this chapter, the popularity of psychology began to emerge in America in the 1920s. It showed such a powerful application of science to the solving of our problems that people were fascinated with it.

The problem with popular psychology, or Pop Psychology, is that myths can be perpetuated because although the idea being stated may be enticing, exciting and have a sort of "face validity" (meaning it seems to be obvious and it seems to make sense), there is no substance of support for the concept in the literature of the field.

Consider some of these areas that we often hold to be true:

Visualize having achieved your dreams.

Although this concept is supported in many self-help books, research suggests that this visualization may actually reduce your motivation! This is different than the more effective practice of visualizing yourself actually doing the things you need to do to reach your goals!

Personal empowerment.

This is a popular one. The premise is similar to visualizing your achieved dream, and is just as ineffective. Personal empowerment is not a "feeling" it is all about having influence on our environment and on the people in it. Again, it is all about doing something, not just visualizing it or feeling it.

Change happens when you are ready.

Truth is, change happens when a person experiences that they cost of their behavior outweighs the benefit of their behavior. This is a complex decision point. Admittedly there may be a point at which the person is ready to "see" this, but ultimately the rational mind can evaluate the costs and benefits and come to a rational decision to change at any time.

Positive thinking.

Positive thinking is helpful, but it must be accompanied by a realistic appraisal of the situation at hand. The fault of this perspective is that it often makes the claim that if you think positively about something, it will get better. This is distinct from the acceptance of your situation with grace and the discovery of the peace that accompanies that.

Want some more myths about Popular Psychology?

50 Myths in Popular Psychology

Learning Outcomes

Upon completion of this Chapter, students should be able to:

1. Discuss the moral and ethical considerations of the experiments with Little Albert.

2. Cite the research methods and discipline Watson insisted upon to ensure that Psychology remained an objective science.

Teaching

John B. Watson (1878-1958)

The book opens this chapter with the startling, yet very famous story, of Little Albert. Keep in mind that up un-

 MOVIE - Baby Albert Experiments ———

——— Mystery Solved - We now know what happened to
Little Albert!

til this time, there were really no specific guidelines for experimental use of humans in studies. We would be hard pressed to get the OK to condition a small child to fear objects today.

Watson's published works and advocacy for a more pragmatic, behavioral approach to Psychology was welcomed by a good many other psychologists. He promoted real world applications of psychology to solve real world problems. After his scandalous affair and dismissal from his professor position, Watson found himself in the career he would hold until his retirement, advertising. Along with this, Watson wrote about and influenced a great number of areas in applied psychology:

1. Advertising.
2. Consumer research.
3. Child raising practices - where he advocated for a rather objective approach rather than permissive parenting.

Behaviorism

Watson attacked the field of psychology and advocated that it focus on being a purely objective, natural science. To this end, Watson advocated for the use of the following methods:

1. Observation with or without the use of instruments.
2. Testing methods.
3. The verbal report method. (Watson supported the use of verbal reports despite being against the process of introspection!)
4. The conditioned reflex method.

The focus of this behaviorism was on the reactions of the subject that could be recorded objectively. Muscular movements, glandular secretions, anything that could be reduced to simple *Stimulus/Response* relationships. Watson referred to more complex behaviors and "acts" but felt they could all be reduced to simple *Stimulus/Re-*

sponse relationships. His goal was to move psychology as a science with methods as objective as those used in physics.

Instincts

Although he agreed with the concept of instincts earlier in his career, he later rejected the notion. He went to the extreme to support the notion that there is no genetic component to behavior; all is traceable to social learning from early childhood.

Emotions

No different than any other behavior, Watson felt that emotions were simply responses to stimuli. Each emotions is associated with a particular pattern of physiological responses. This was in direct contradiction to the theories of emotion by William James, who suggested that emotions arise from our interpretation of stimuli (what is known today as the "cognitive appraisal theory" of emotions.

This brings us to Watson's work with Little Albert. Watson set out to demonstrate that emotions, such as fear, could be conditioned or taught. That phobias actually arose from early conditioned fear responses.

Cognition

Even cognition, the very act of thinking, was reduced by Watson. He felt that thought was simply a process of self-talking that reflected in the muscle movements in our face. (Interestingly enough, while this reduction of the thinking process has been largely rejected in mainstream science, the notion of processing information using sub-voice, or talking to one's self does make another appearance. Vygotsky, the famous Russian psychologist famous for "scaffolding" and "zone of proximal development" emphasized the function of "private speech" as an essential component of learning...such as when we talk ourselves through a complex math problem.)

Lev Vygotsky (1896-1934)

Why was this all so popular?

People were disenchanted with old ideas of myth, customs, and convention. Watson offered a scientific way to approach human behavior. The popularity of Behaviorism was so powerful that it was often supported with the same fervor of religious ideas. His work empowered people to feel that they cold impact others' behavior. He went so far as to say that given control over the entire environment of a small child he could turn them into a "doctor, lawyer, artist, merchant-chief, and, yes, even beggar-man and thief."

It is instructive to read the section in the book on the debate which took place between Watson and McDougall. McDougall won the day, behaviorism continued to be popular, but the stage was set for the future of psychology and the humanists.

Psychology Becomes Popular

This kind of scientific approach to applied psychology created a great spirit of hope. The kind of hope associated with "positivism" the notion that we are a smart species and we can solve our problems.

Joseph Jastrow was a psychologist whose writings about psychology in popular magazines was instrumental in supporting this popularity. He had a column called "Keeping Mentally Fit" which was syndicated in 150 newspapers.

Joseph Jastrow (1863-1944)

In one of his articles, Jastrow made the argument that perception is both a sensory and cognitive process. To support that premise, he introduced a now famous "reversible figure" known as the "Duck-Rabbit."

Duck-Rabbit

Jastrow can be considered the father of the self-help book movement with his column, his manual titled "Piloting your Life: The Psychologist as Helmsman," and his frequent articles for *Popular Science Monthly*, *Cosmopolitan*, and *Harper's*.

Assessment

Chapter 10 Discussion - Experiments

Consider the experiments with Little Albert. Discuss what ethical concerns you may have about this experiment. Review the website on "10 Psychological Experiments that Could Never Happen Again." Consider if the information learned from these experiments is valuable enough to justify the methods.

Chapter 10 Quiz

1. Describe the experimental methods that Watson supported/demanded in order to assure that Psychology was an objective science.

Behaviorism: After the Founding

11

Attention

Do violent video games impact youth?

In this chapter you are going to learn a bit about the work of Alfred Bandura. Bandura is famous for many things, among them the Bobo Doll Experiments where he demonstrated that children will imitate violent behavior by watching roll models exhibit this behavior on TV.

The original study was flawed by the fact that, well, the use of a Bobo Doll. The purpose of the Bobo Doll is to hit it, so maybe THAT is why kids were likely to hit the doll!

Additional research has been conducted, however, aimed and determining the degree to which video games actually change behavior. It is important to recognize that video games are not the only or most important predictor of violence (family violence, anger-prone personality, rejection from peers, poverty, and school problems are all risk factors as well.)

Is this different than teaching a young child to hunt?

Bobo Doll However, the evidence does link video games with later aggression. Research on the impact on de-sensitization does identify a link, but it is among those who may already show some of these tendencies, so it enhances them. Interestingly, those with a cooperative personality who play networked video games show a higher propensity to cooperating after they play!

It seems that video games impact depends greatly on the individual who is playing the game. The decision to restrict or allow kids to play these games should be mad eon a case by case basis. The distraction of video games, at the expense of grades and exercise may be more important issues to address.

The Truth about Violent Video Games and Kids

Technical Report on the Review of Violent Video Game
Literature

Learning Outcomes

Upon completion of this Chapter, students should be able to:

1. Differentiate between respondent conditioning (Pavlov) and operant conditioning (Skinner).

2. Identify how Bandura and Rotter reintroduce the utility of cognition in behaviorism.

3. Discuss the results of a test for Locus of Control on behavior.

Teaching

Three Stages of Behaviorism

This development of this most important school of thought was brought about in three stages:

1. Watson's behaviorism - The Law of Effect

2. Neo-behaviorism - Includes the work of Hull and Skinner. Shared many beliefs with Watson, including:

    1. The core of psychology is the study of learning.

    2. Most behavior, no matter how complex, can be accounted for by the laws of conditioning.

    3. Psychology must adopt the principle of operationism.

3. Socio-behaviorism - This included the work of Bandura and Rotter and represents a return to the importance of cognition in behavior (within a behavioral framework.

Operationism

Operationism advocated for the adoption of terminology to be used in psychology that was objective and reflected what could be directly observed. The term is somewhat analogous to "operationalizing" which is the process of defining, in precise ways, how you are going to measure a particular construct. In a study on intelligence and academic achievement, for instance, we would have to "operationalize" how we are going to measure intelligence and how we are going to measure academic achievement (because there is more than one way to measure intelligence and more than one way to measure achievement.)

Edward Chase Tolman (1886-1959)

Edward Tolman expanded upon the work of Watson with his purposive behaviorism model. This was not to say that he had adopted a sense of "purpose" for behavior that would arise from consciousness (he rejected this)...it was thus titled to point out that while all behavior can be defined objectively within the behavioral framework, all behavior was also goal directed.

Edward Tolman holding a rat

It can be said, however, that consciousness is evoked in this notion. At least to the extent that the organism, be it a rat or a human, has within them a concept of the goal and that this concept persists to maintain the behavior that will lead to that goal.

Tolman described his theory in terms of the variables that impact behavior. He listed 5 independent variables as the cause of behavior in a Stimulus/Response fashion:

1. Environmental stimuli.

2. Physiological drives.

3. Heredity.

4. Previous training.

5. Age

However, he also identified that there were unobservable factors that occur within the individual that actually cause the behavior. So the relationship between the S (stimulus) and the R (response) is the processing of the organism (O).

S-R becomes S-O-R

This recognition of the cognitive factors of the organism in this equation places Tolman as one of the first Cognitive Psychologists.

Clark Leonard Hull (1884-1952)

Hull's influence on the world of psychology was profound. He brought a new level of mathematics and logic to the study of behavior. He had a lifelong interest in objective scientific methodology and functional laws.

Early in his career he studied such varied topics as the effects of tobacco, hypnosis and suggestibility, created tests and measurements, published a book on aptitude testing, and built a machine to calculate correlations.

Hull and the Concept of Hypotheses

Hull introduced the notion, within his scientific method, of **hypothetical deductive method.**

Hull's Correlation Machine - Image from Wikipedia

Hull's Biography that includes his varied methods and his machine.

Essentially, he introduced the notion of deducing a set of ideas about the relationship between factors prior to beginning a study, and then setting about to collect information about the described relationship. Ultimately, Hull's concept of learning, his hypothesis, supported the notion that all motivation arose from physiological **drives**, both complex and basic. In his **Law of Primary Reinforcement** happens when we first encounter the relationship between these stimuli. As we continue to encounter this relationship we form **habits** that describe the deep and long lasting patterns of our behavior.

Learning could not occur without reinforcement, according to Hull.

B.F. Skinner (1904-1990)

Skinner is one of the best known psychologists in the world. His behavioral model has become one of the most successful theories ever when applied to education and to clinical psychology. The concept of "it just works" is very apt to describe the operant conditioning model that he conceived.

When we are first introduced to the field of Psychology, we may encounter a list of "goals" for the field. These include the following:

B.F. Skinner

1. **Describe behavior** - using objective accurate and accepted terms to describe behavior.

2. **Explain behavior** - models and theories that explain the relationships among variables.

3. **Predict behavior** - the use of these models and theories to predict behavior when we have knowledge of a set of these variables.

4. **Control Behavior** - manipulate the behaviors by manipulating the controlling variables in accordance with the models and theories.

There is no model in Psychology that has better met each of these goals than Skinner's Behaviorism. Skinner himself states that he just set out to describe behavior, but he ended up explaining it, and providing the tools to both predict and control behavior.

Skinner never denied the existence of an inner world or cognition. He just felt that it was not useful in the study of behavior. When I learned of this theory, the human mind (all of cognition, feelings, motivations, etc.) could be considered a "black box", the contents of which we may never fully understand. We can, however, still understand the relationship between what Skinner called antecedents and consequences and their impact of behavior.

According to Skinner, we simply need to study the relationship between inputs and outputs in order to understand behavior. Understanding the mind, represented by the black box, is not that important.

Another important aspect of the work of Skinner is the fact that he did not really feel the need to generate data using large sets of subjects. He felt that the result of this type of work resulted in conclusions as to what the "average" person might do, which is of no use to the individual. Behaviorism is, ultimately a very personal and individual thing.

Operant Conditioning

Operant conditioning is best explained using a modern formulation of it called the **A-B-C Contingency Theory**.

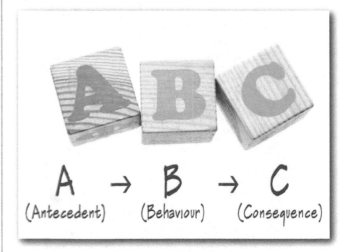

The A, and the B, and the C in this equation describe the ways in which Antecedent factors (things that lead up to the behavior) and Consequences (the resulting reinforcement or punishment - think Law of Effect) "operate" on or impact Behavior. Essentially, by deeply understanding the As and the Cs, we can produce the Bs.

Schedules of Reinforcement

One of the most powerful products of Skinner's work had to do with schedules of reinforcement. Skinner was able to demonstrate that different rates of reinforcement changed the **strength** and **durability** of the behavior. One of his most profound discoveries was that intermittent reinforcement actually produced more stable responses than did continuous reinforcement (a reinforcer after every event of the response.)

Here are some of the alternate schedules of behavior that have been developed and used to manage behavior in both animals and humans. (I will use the example of a mouse pressing a lever to receive a food pellet as an example.)

1. **Fixed Ratio** - this system delivers a reinforcer after the occurrence of a fixed number of responses - each time a mouse presses the lever 4 times, it gets a food pellet.

2. **Variable Ratio** - this system delivers a reinforcer based on a changing number of responses - a mechanism is set up to reinforce the mouse with a food pellet after a randomly selected number of responses between 1-10, at first the mouse get one after 4 responses, then 2, then 6, then 8, etc.

3. **Fixed Interval** - this system delivers a reinforcer if the behavior occurs at least once within a specified time - the mouse receives a food pellet once per minute as long as the lever is pressed some time during that minute.

4. **Variable Interval** - similar to variable ratio, this system varies the time from the fixed interval.

5. **Fixed Duration** - this system delivers a reinforcer if the behavior occurs for a specific duration of time - a mouse would have to continually press the lever for a full 30 seconds to get a food pellet.

6. **Variable Duration** - this system varies the amount of time the behavior needs to happen.

The important take-away in all of this is that the systems that use variable schedules produce more consistent behavior patterns and these behaviors are less vulnerable to **extinction** (the behavior going away after the reinforcement stops) than the fixed systems.

To understand the influence of this work from Skinner one need only go to Las Vegas and watch the slot machines deliver rewards on a variable ratio basis!

Shaping Behavior

Another concept of Skinner has to do with the shaping of behavior through reinforcement of progressively more accurate attempts at the target behavior. This is how Skinner attempts to explain the learning of complex behaviors such as speaking. Our young children might not get their first words right the fist time but we are calling Grandma the first time they say anything even remotely close to Mom or Dad! The child is thrilled by the reaction of those around them and attempts to do more...thus we progressively shape the sounds a child makes into words.

Skinner's Apparatuses

If you recall from the text, Skinner was a tinkerer. Throughout his career he built things. One of the most famous things that he created was called the **Skinner Box**. This apparatus allowed Skinner to teach rats a variety of responses to stimuli and shape very complex behaviors.

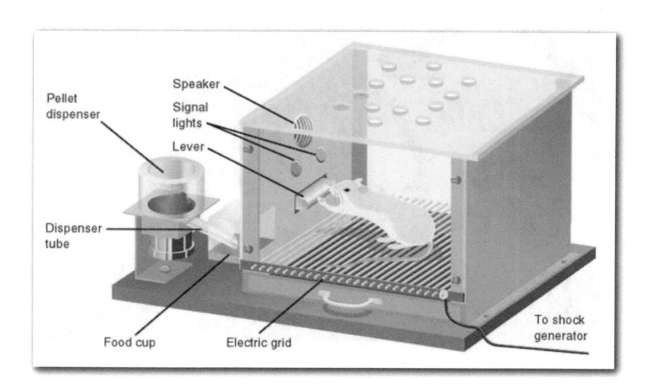

Pellet dispenser

Speaker

Signal lights

Lever

Dispenser tube

Food cup

Electric grid

To shock generator

A pigeon being placed into its compartment in the guidance system of a warhead.

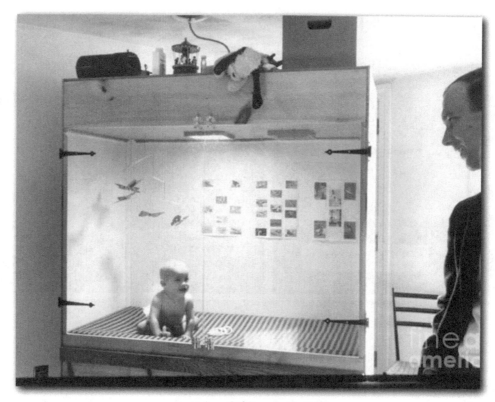

A version of Skinner's Air Crib

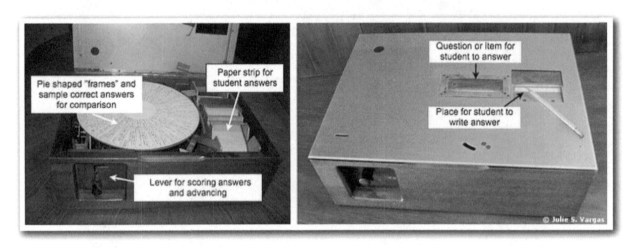

Skinner's Teaching Machine

Preparing for the birth of their second child, Skinner created a mechanized **Air Crib** to relieve parents of the menial tasks during the first two years. Skinner's daughter was raised in it for two years and seems to have suffered no ill effects!

With a shortage of teachers, ample students, and a need to keep up with the science of the Russians, Skinner found an eager audience for his **Teaching Machines** which automated some aspects of teaching. While Skinner's machines were somewhat crude, they are not unlike the current use of teaching software and computers used in schools today.

Finally, one of the most bizarre applications of operant conditioning has Skinner assisting the military in developing the first self-guiding, smart bomb. The brain of the smart bombs however, were pigeons. The military was unimpressed, and they pigeons were overjoyed!

Today we have applications of Skinner's **Operant Conditioning** model in the form of such interventions as **Behavior Management, Applied Behavior Analysis,** and **Cognitive Behavior Therapy.** It cannot be stressed enough that these applications have been some of the most successful approaches to psychotherapy.

Albert Bandura (1925-) and Social Cognitive Theory

Albert Bandura Timeline by Ciara Walker

Bandura provides a less extreme form of behaviorism that also leaves room for the concept of cognition to come back into the conversation. The essence of his theory is as follows:

Bandura felt that we did not learn all that we know through automated triggers to external stimuli. We are actively engaged in learning from our environment and we learn specific behaviors by observing others and by observing the reinforcement they receive for their behavior. He called this **vicarious reinforcement**. A person can then self-regulate their behavior by choosing to act the same way and thus open the opportunity to receive the same reinforcer.

However, just as in behaviorism, if the reinforcer is not provided, the behavior can go extinct. (Although Bandura did not dismiss the notion of self-reinforcement inside the mind!)

Bandura did a lot of work on the power of role models. Noting that television and movies included much more violence, Bandura set out to explore if watching violent behavior led to acting out. While his famous Bobo Doll research was flawed, he did find a relationship and through better designed studies did conclude that there is a relationship between the violence that someone watches on TV and in movies (and video games) and actual behavior.

Albert Bandura

MOVIE - Bobo Doll Experiment on Aggression

The last concept to cover here is Bandura's concept of **self-efficacy**. Self efficacy is a person's perception as to their own abilities to accomplish a task. We sometimes call it confidence.

Bandura recognized that as individuals approach a difficult task, there is a cognitive appraisal going on as to how the person feels about accomplishing this task. If they feel they have the skill (and their self-perception is correct) they will likely perform better. This is a little bit of science behind the idea of "believing in yourself."

Jullian Rotter (1916-2014)

In slight contrast to Bandura, Rotter asserts that the role of cognition is much more central to what he termed **Social Learning Theory**. His theory asserted the following ideas:

1. We form subjective expectations of the outcomes or results of our behavior in terms of the amount and kind of reinforcement likely to follow it.

2. We estimate the likelihood that behaving in a certain way leads to a specific reinforcement and adjust our behavior accordingly.

3. We place different values on different reinforcers and assess their relative worth for different situations.

4. Because each of us functions in a psychological environment that is unique to us as individuals, the same reinforcement can have different values for different people.

Rotter also introduced a very valuable concept to our understanding of behavior, **Locus of Control**. Locus of control asserts that we interpret our fate to be either due to internal factors in our own control (Internal Locus of Control) or that we are at the whim of factors outside of ourselves and our control (External Locus of Control).

Rotter's research has shown that people with Internal Locus of Control seem to be happier, healthier, get better grades, are more popular and socially skilled, and are better able to cope with stress than those who exhibit External Locus of Control.

Assessment

Chapter 11 Discussion - Control

Locus of Control and Attribution Style Test

Take the Locus of Control and Attribution Style test. Discuss your results. Identify patterns in your own behavior that are impacted by this. Relate stories of people you know who you feel have a different Locus of Control than you do.

Chapter 11 Quiz

1. Describe both respondent conditioning (Pavlov) and operant conditioning (Skinner). Compare and contrast these two viewpoints on behavior (explain the similarities and differences.)

2. Write a brief essay as to the contributions made by Bandura and Rotter in reintroducing cognition into behaviorism.

Gestalt Psychology

12

Attention

Gestalt and Optical Illusions

The Gestalt school of thought introduced a number of concepts related to perception of stimuli. These "rules" that our brain follows allow us to experience consistencies in our world and enhance our functioning. These same rules can be used, however, by clever artists to make your brain see things that are not there.

The 3rd Dimension - Notice how all the pictures in this book have "shadows" giving you the illusion that they are slightly lifted up from the page!

Color Constancy - In this image, the color of the square marked with an "A" is the same as the square marked with a "B"...I have a printed version of this diagram to prove it!

MOVIE - "Can you find the sniper"

Learning Outcomes

Upon completion of this Chapter, students should be able to:

1. Explain the concept embodied in the phrase, "the whole is greater than the sum of its parts."

2. Document examples of perceptual organization and perceptual constancies as they exist in the environment.

Teaching

The Gestalt Revolt

The difference between Gestalt Psychology and the other contemporary approaches was simple. The Gestalt folks accepted the value of consciousness. They also fought against the notion that all of our existence can be broken down into bits that are associated with each other or simple responses to stimuli.

The best examples of this antithesis to the deconstruction of our experience lay in sensory experience. When we see a tree, we don't see the trunk, the branches, the leaves and then construct these separate pieces together and form a tree, we experience the tree all at once in all its "treeness." Similarly, in music we can hear notes but when we chain them together they form a melody and that melody is not an inherent part of the quality of each note.

From here we get the most famous quote to summarize Gestalt: **the whole is greater than the sum of its parts.**

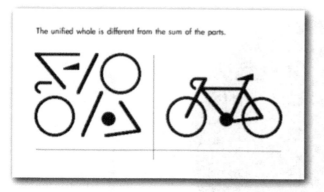

The unified whole is different from the sum of the parts.

The German philosopher, **Immanuel Kant** (1724-1804), wrote that while we experience stimuli in all its pieces, the mind is very adept at creating patterns and forms out of these various pieces. We can experience this tendency throughout human history when we recognize that the constellations in the night sky are a product of this process. There is no inherent order of the stars to create these images, it is our minds that see the images that are there. Consider the image below and all the different interpretations of the patterns that exist around the start Betelgeuse (our constellation Orion, and yes, the movie character BeetleJuice is a play on this!)

Other thinkers contributed to the thoughts of the Gestalt Psychologists including **Franz Brentano** (1838-1917) (we should focus on studying the experience of something rather than the elements of the something), **Ernest Mach** (1838-1916) (a physicist who posited that patterns we experience such as geometric shapes and melodies form space-time sensations that are independent of their individual parts), **Christian Von Ehrenfels** (1859-1932) proposed that some qualities of an experience cannot be explained by understanding its parts, and even **William James** embraced the notion that we experience objects as whole objects.

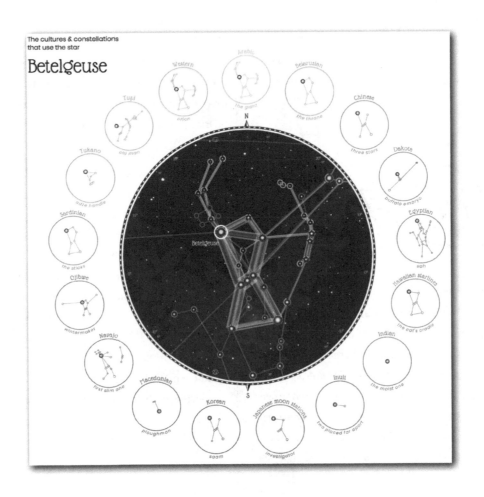

The cultures & constellations
that use the star

Betelgeuse

Max Wertheimer (1880-1943)

Wertheimer founded the journal **Psychological Research**, which became the journal of Gestalt Psychology school of thought.

Max Wertheimer

Publication was suspended in Nazi Germany but continued once the war was over. Wertheimer expressed a specific goal to create the Gestalt theory.

Wertheimer made a strong impression on an American student of his, **Abraham Maslow**. Maslow went on to develop his hierarchy of needs, self-actualization, and found the Humanist Psychology school of thought.

Kurt Koffka (1886-1941)

Koffka's introduction of Gestalt psychology to the American audience might have done more bad than good. He included the word "perception" in the title and the American audience took this to mean that the application of Gestalt had only to do with perception. This, in fact, continues to be perceived because it is so easy to demonstrate the concepts of "whole is greater than the sum of its parts" using images. The truth is that Gestalt applies to all of human experience and has a focus on thinking and learning.

Consider the act of making a decision on which class to take in a given semester. You might break down all of the elements of the decision into different parts (time, days, work, childcare, hobbies, sleeping, balance, favorite TV shows, etc.) but ultimately you at some time sit back and perceive the greater wide angle view of your decision, how is this going to work? That is Gestalt.

Wolfgang Köhler (1887-1967)

Regarded as the most prolific promoter of Gestalt Psychology, Köhler's writings were done with precision and care and became standard works on Gestalt.

Köhler's work began by observing ape behavior. He observed that apes learned and applied their minds to problem solving in ways very similar to humans.

Wolfgang Köhler

Köhler found that the Gestalt perspective was a natural aspect of the nature of things. To his credit, Köhler was one of very few non-Jewish protestors against the treatment of Jews by the Nazis.

Perceptual Constancies

Giving over to the notion that Gestalt has to do solely with perception, we are going to discuss **perceptual constancies**. Perceptual constancies, a tenant of the field of Gestalt, identifies the experience we have with the sensation of certain objects. We have a tendency to attribute the same characteristics to an object, even when we view it from different perspectives.

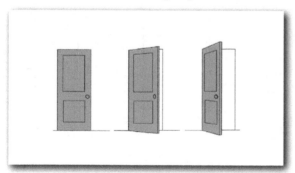

Even through the image on your retina of these doors changes from rectangle to trapezoid, in your mind the door retains its original shape of rectangle

This concept applies to many aspects of our perception including size constancy (an object moving away from us does not actually get smaller), and color constancy (changes in light and shadow do not change the actual color of something).

Principles of Organization

Another set of principles set forth by Gestalt Psychology include a list of ways in which we observe and interpret stimuli. The following is taken right from our text:

Proximity. Parts that are close together in time or space appear to belong together and tend to be perceived together. (In the figure below you see the circles in groups and the squares in the form of a cross.)

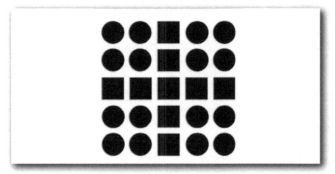

Continuity. There is a tendency in our perception to follow a direction, to connect the elements in a way that makes them seem continuous or flowing in a particular direction. (In the figure below, you tend to see the curved line as a continuous line rather than the "gravestone" shaped objects.)

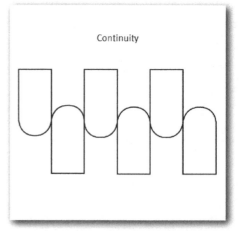

Image from BC Open Textbooks

Similarity. Similar parts tend to be seen together as forming a group. (In the figure below, we tend to group the black circles together and the red circles together. We might see then we we watch a professional football game and note the distribution of fans for both teams by color.)

Image from Smashing Magazine

Closure. There is a tendency in our perception to complete incomplete figures, to fill in gaps. (In the figure below, you can perceive a number of objects and we perceive them as complete...we see a black triangle and three circles partially hidden below a white triangle that is not even there!)

Simplicity. We tend to see a figure as being as good as possible under the stimulus conditions; the Gestalt psychologists called this prägnanz, or good form. A good Gestalt is symmetrical, simple, and stable and cannot be made simpler or more orderly. (In the figure below we have a tendency to see the circle, triangle, and rectangle in the left image because it makes it easier to understand the image.)

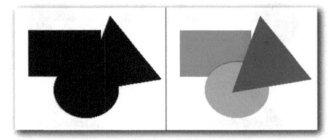

Figure/ground. We tend to organize perceptions into the object being looked at (the figure) and the background against which it appears (the ground). The figure seems to be more substantial and to stand out from its background. (In the figure below we see the apple with a bite taken out of it, and then we can see the profile of Steve Jobs. These are called reversible images and there are lots of examples of these.)

Gestalt and the Learning Process

For a moment, we revisit the work of Köhler. His observations of the perceptual abilities of chimpanzees and how they solved problems illuminated both the limitations of chimpanzees and of people. In both cases, Köhler professed that when a problem is perceived and the objects in the environment are combined to provide a solution the experience is called **insight**. We use this word to describe a similar experience when make connections between non-physical ideas as well.

Key to Köhler's interpretation of these observations was that this sort of problem solving was different than simple trial and error. There was a degree of processing going on in the mind.

Productive Thinking in Humans

I find the section on Productive Thinking to be very interesting. Wertheimer published the notion that humans develop the ability to see a problem in its wholeness over time. Different problems will demand a different degree of seeing this Gestalt. This is seemingly the same as the notion of creative (divergent) and algorithmic (convergent) thinking processes.

Productive Learning was seen as the process by which the "whole problem" dominates the parts. Learning by repetition has its place, but learning through the development of insight into problem solving was much more powerful and lasting.

A thought just occurred to me. When I was growing up a product called "Hooked on Phonics" came out. This was a language teaching process that broke down the elements of language into small sounds that could be easily learned. The developers felt that this was the best way to learn language. This would have definitely NOT been a Gestalt approach!

The opposition to this was the "whole language" school of thought that proposed that the best way to learn language was in conversations and reading, experiencing language in the way it is usually experienced. In the end, the Phonics perspective won out and we see lots of early childhood education language tools based on this.

If, according to Wertheimer, we develop the ability to see things from a wider, Gestalt perspective, could it be that while Phonics works for language development in early life, whole language approaches (such as emersion programs - where you go to a class or even a place where the language you are trying to learn is the only one that can be used.) could work better for older people attempting to learn a new language.

Kurt Lewin (1890-1947) and Field Theory

Kurt Lewin

Lewin had some knowledge of field theory as it was applied in physics. Lewin's theory was that psychology could be described in the same manner. He called this field the **Life Space** and populated it with the our past, present and future experiences, knowledge, and influences. Each of these is purported to have an impact on our behavior.

Lewin proposed the use of a topology map to diagram behaviors and the factors that influence them. He would use lines to connect concepts and arrows to depict the direction of a goal and supporting/opposing forces.

Assessment

Chapter 12 Quiz

1. Explain the concept embodied in the phrase, "the whole is greater than the sum of its parts."

Chapter 12 Assignment - Gestalt

Purpose

The purpose of this assignment is for you to learn how to recognize examples of Gestalt perception that occur in the real world. Many of the graphics that are used to teach about Gestalt are manufactured for simplicity, but these concepts were first observed in the real world as psychologists wondered about how we perceive the world.

Skills and Knowledge

You will demonstrate the following skills and knowledge by completing this assignment:

1. Develop a deep understanding of at least two different Gestalt perception rules.

2. Identify the existence of Gestalt perception in the real world

3. Write a title page and paper in a word processor.

4. Pasting images into a digital document.

5. Upload the paper to the assignment drop box.

Task

The text and this book provide a number of examples of the Gestalt principles of perception. For this assignment you are going to explore your environment and find (or create) two examples of these principles in action!

Paste the images into your document and then provide the name of the Gestalt rule and a brief explanation of the image and how it demonstrates the rule.

Criteria for Success

Use the rubric below as a guide to this assignment.

Title Page   10 points

Standard title page with name, date, course, college name and the name of the assignment.

Perceptual Constancy   20 points

The picture portrays either size, shape, or color constancy

Essay   10 points

Write a brief paragraph describing how the image portrays the Perceptual Constancy.

Perceptual Organization   10 points

The picture portrays an example of one of the following organizing features: proximity, continuity, similarity, closure, simplicity, or figure/ground.

Essay   10 points

Write a brief paragraph describing how the image portrays the Perceptual Organization

Mechanics   10 points

Spelling, syntax, and organizational structure of the paper. Clear and organized.

Psychoanalysis: The Beginning

13

Attention

The Emmanuel Church Healing Movement

From 1904 until his retirement in 1929, the Rev. Dr. Elwood Worcester served as Minister at the Emmanuel Church in Boston. At the time, Medical Psychiatry based its methods on mental illness being a physical illness. Having had success in providing treatment and support for persons with tuberculosis, Worcester though the same methods may work on the "nervously and morally diseased."

Preliminary meetings developed into "Weekly Health Conferences." Each meeting began with hymns and prayers, and was followed by a lecture by a physician or member of the clergy. The techniques of suggestion and auto-suggestion were used but the methods were eclectic.

Suggestion, simply put, was providing guidance as one explores another's feelings, thoughts and behaviors.

Auto-suggestion would entail having the person do this for themselves. This is about as close as it is going to get to modern psychotherapy!

Emmanuel Church in Boston

Four components made up the primary approach to therapy. The church continued to offer large lectures and classes, primarily devoted to what would now be termed "functional" illness. There was a clinic, held un-der the auspices of the church and staffed by physicians, which offered some traditional medical care. The third component, unique at the time, offered the services of "lay therapists" who were trained on the job. Treatment consisted of a relatively brief form of analysis, support and direction for making changes in the patient's life, and the use of suggestion to relieve symptoms. Therapy was reinforced by volunteers who visited the patients at home.

It is remarkable how closely this resembles much of what gos on in psychiatric rehabilitation today.

Learning Outcomes

Upon completion of this Chapter, students should be able to:

1. Describe the importance of free association, resistance, and repression in clinical settings.

2. Describe the relationship between the id, ego, and super-ego.

3. Discuss the use of defense mechanisms.

Teaching

Three Shocks

Freud is known for stating that the history of human kind has experienced three significant shocks:

1. Copernicus - when he described that the Earth is not the center of the universe but one of many planets that orbit the Sun.

2. Darwin - when he demonstrated that we are not a unique and separate species of creation but evolved from lower beings.

3. Freud (himself) - when he announced that we are truly not as rational as we like to believe but we are under the influence of unconscious forces that we have very little control over.

There is some truth to these assertions. When Freud entered the scene, much of the old historical structuralism and functionalism were history, Gestalt was just in the process of transferring itself from Germany to the

US, and Behaviorism was all the rage in the United States.

Antecedents to Psychoanalysis

1. **Philosophical speculations about unconscious psychological phenomena**

    1. Still mostly centered on perception of stimuli, Leibnitz and Herbert identified levels of perception, some of which were within our awareness while others were below our consciousness, or in our unconscious.

    2. Fechner stated that the mind is like an iceberg, with most of it "below the surface." This imagery will appear again when we look at Freud's theory of Personality.

2. **Early ideas about psychopathology**

    1. The history of the treatment of mental illness, particularly in the later Christian era, is filled with horrors, torture, and executions.

    2. Vives (Spain), Pinel (France), and Dorothea Dix (US) all advocated for a more humane treatment of those with mental illness.

    3. Benjamin Rush, a signer on the Declaration of Independence, was the first person to open a formal practice and hospital for mental illness. Unfortunately he is also the founder of a form of "shock therapy" that entailed dunking patients into ice water.

    4. Talk therapy was introduced, surprisingly, through the Emmanuel Church Healing Movement, which supported psychotherapy as a way to help persons with mental illness.

    5. Hypnosis was formalized and used to treat hysteria.

3. **Evolutionary theory**

    1. Darwin discussed many topics in his writing that became part of the theory of psycho-

analysis. These topics include, unconscious mental processes and conflicts, significance of dreams, hidden symbolism in certain behaviors, and the importance of sexual arousal.

2. Those who elaborated on Darwin's writings included thoughts about the evolution of the human mind and the evidence of a "sex drive" at a very young age.

Sigmund Freud (1856-1939) and Psychoanalysis

Freud is arguably the best known person in psychology in the world. He was, by training, a medical doctor, but his interests in philosophy and classical literature were intense.

Working as a medical doctor, he was introduced to the case of Anna O., a patient of a colleague of his, and his interactions in this case launched his study of Psychoanalysis.

Sigmund Freud

Freud's colleague had identified the processes of the "talking cure" and the concept of **transference** which would later figure very great in Freud's theory. Transference is when we transfer our feelings for one person to another. In the case of Anna O., she transferred her feelings for her father to the therapist. This was seen as a positive outcome as various reports show that her symptoms lessened when this happened.

Sigmund Freud Timeline by Mark Kavanaugh

Free Association

Freud stopped using hypnosis as a way to get at the underlying causes of disturbances and instead turned to a process he termed **free association**. Freud would encourage his patients to lay on his couch and simply say anything that came to mind. The goal of this process was to release repressed memories and thoughts that were assumed to be the cause of the mental illness.

Bertha Pappenheim (Anna O.)

This image of Freud sitting by the couch while his patients talk is likely the most famous portrayal of Freud.

Freud asserted that the cause of most of neurosis that he was treating involved incidents of traumatic sexual experiences and abuse, usually by family members. He presented his paper and it was not received well by the scientific community of the day. A year later, he reversed his position. He rewrote his paper stating that the traumatic sexual experiences his patients reported were not real, they were fantasies. However, the state- ments from his patients were quite real to them so it mattered little because they had the same effect on the patient.

Today we are unsure why Freud changed his position. It is likely that many of his patients did, indeed, have a real history of trauma. It seems that the scientific community may have not been ready to deal with that.

Dream Analysis

Another method that Freud developed for delving into the unconscious mind was dream analysis. He felt that dreams could be a rich source of emotional material and could lead to a greater understanding of the issues that someone is dealing with.

Freud adopted dream analysis as a basic technique in psychoanalysis.

Sexuality as a Central Theme

Freud later worked with Charcot in Paris where he was exposed to Charcot's thoughts that all of hysteria is an issue about sex or genitals. This became a focal point for Freud's thoughts from this point on. Freud felt that sexuality was the central theme in his theory. He had no tolerance for anyone questioning this position. Despite this stand, Freud grew popular as did his theories.

Psychoanalysis as a Method of Treatment

Freud felt that early childhood experiences (real or imagined) were the source of mental problems. Free association would work to a point but he would often encounter **resistance** when the memories that were being triggered were deemed to be too shameful for recollection.

From this, Freud formulated the basic tenant of **repressed memories**. This idea proposes that if we have a memory or thought that causes too much stress and strain for us to cope, we can allocate it to the unconscious part of the mind.

Using free association, transference, and dream analysis, Freud would search for these hidden memories, convinced that bringing them to the light would help his patients suffering.

Psychoanalysis as a System of Personality

Instincts

Some of the more well known aspects of Freud's work involve his thoughts on the structure of personality. First, Freud contended that humans have just two basic **instincts** (by this Freud meant drives, not animal-type instincts). These two basic drives included one for life and one for death, a life instinct and a death instinct.

The form of energy that manifests the life instinct he called **libido**. The death instinct was characterized by aggression.

CONSCIOUS
LEVEL

PRECONSCIOUS
LEVEL

UNCONSCIOUS
LEVEL

Ego
Executive mediating
between id impulses
and superego
inhibitions; testing
reality; rational.
Operates mainly at
conscious level but also
at preconscious level.

Superego
Ideals and
morals; striving
for perfection;
incorporated from
parents; becoming a
person's conscience.
Operates mostly at
preconscious level.

Id
Basic impulses (sex and aggression);
seeking immediate gratification;
irrational and impulsive.
Operates at unconscious level.

Levels of Personality

Freud believed there were two levels of personality, conscious and unconscious. Similar to Fechner's notion of the mind being like an iceberg, very little of the personality is thought to be conscious (like the tip of the iceberg being above the water.)

Structures of the personality developed through childhood. The **id** represented basic needs and selfish desires and rested entirely in the unconscious. The **ego**, or the "I" is the conscious awareness of the person, the **super-ego** is the representation of learned expectations.

Anxiety

Freud focused a lot of his work on the concept of anxiety.

1. **Objective Anxiety** arose from fear of actual dangers in the world.

2. **Neurotic Anxiety** comes from recognizing the inherent dangers of satisfying id impulses.

3. **Moral Anxiety** is a fear of one's conscience. When we act, or think of acting against our moral standing.

To cope with these anxieties the ego develops what Freud termed **Defense Mechanisms**. These are strategies to divert the energy associated with the anxiety and help the ego cope. Here are the ones listed in our text.

1. **Denial** - Denying the existence of an external threat or traumatic event; for example, a person living with a terminal illness may deny the imminence of death.

2. **Displacement** - Shifting id impulses from a threatening or unavailable object to an object that is available, such as replacing hostility toward one's boss with hostility toward one's child.

3. **Projection** - Attributing a disturbing impulse to someone else, such as saying you do not really hate your professor but that he or she hates you.

4. **Rationalization** - Reinterpreting behavior to make it more acceptable and less threatening, such as saying the job from which you were fired was not really a good job anyway.

5. **Reaction Formation** - Expressing an id impulse that is the opposite of the one that is driving the person. For example, someone disturbed by sexual longings may become a crusader against pornography.

6. **Regression** - Retreating to an earlier, less frustrating period of life and displaying the childish and dependent behaviors characteristic of that more secure time.

7. **Repression** - Denying the existence of something that causes anxiety, such as involuntarily removing from consciousness some memory or perception that brings discomfort.

8. **Sublimation** - Altering or displacing id impulses by diverting instinctual energy into socially acceptable behaviors, such as diverting sexual energy into artistically creative behaviors.

Psychosexual Stages of Development

Freud is also considered the "Father of Developmental Psychology" as he was the first to popularize a stage theory through which children go as they develop their id, ego, and super-ego relations. It also traces the location and focus of **libido**. It is important to keep in mind that when Freud talked about infant sexuality, he was talking about the presence of libido, which in adolescence would mature into sexuality.

Freud's Psychosexual Stages of Development

Stages	Ages	Description	Problems/Fixation
Oral Stage	Birth to 2 years	Pleasure from oral stimulation – tasting & sucking	Dependency or aggression; Problems with drinking, smoking, eating, nail biting
Anal Stage	15 months to 3 years	Primary focus on controlling bladder and bowels – eliminating/retaining feces	Anal-expulsive (messy, wasteful, destructive) vs. Anal-retentive (orderly, rigid, obsessive)
Phallic Stage	3 – 6	Primary focus is on genitals – differences between male and female Child becomes rival for the affection of opposite-sex parent – (Oedipus complex) Child begins to identify with the same-sex parent	Fixation can result in sexual deviancies or confused sexual identity Freud believed that girls continued to possess feelings of envy or inferiority – penis envy
Latency Stage	6 to puberty	Sexual desires pushed to background Focus on intellectual and social pursuits	Important stage for development of communication skills and self-confidence
Genital Stage	Puberty through Adulthood	Sexual desires renewed – seek relationships with others	Problems that emerge in this stage are carried over from earlier stages

Assessment

Chapter 13 Discussion - Defenses

You have been introduced to a set of Defense Mechanisms in this chapter. Describe personal experiences that you have had using or seeing these used in the real world.

Chapter 13 Quiz

1. Define and describe the importance of free association, resistance, and repression in clinical settings.

2. Describe the relationship between the id, ego, and super-ego.

Psychoanalysis: After the Founding

14

Attention

Act as If

Adlerian Counseling theory proposes an interesting approach to personal change. It is called the "As If" technique. The individual works with a counselor to identify the key characteristics that are part of the person they want to be. The more clear these characteristics are stated (particularly in behavioral terms) the more effective the technique.

At that point, the individual simply decides to start **acting as if** these were true. Through this process, the individual encounters the challenges and rewards of being that type of person. In a behavioral sense, the world starts to reinforce the behavior.

An alternative to this, particularly if clients are reluctant to put the behaviors into practice is **Reflective As If** technique. This allows the individual to visualize the enactment of the behaviors and speculate on the consequences of them.

Phase 1

At the beginning, the counselor will pose reflective questions:

1. If you were acting as if you were the person you would like to be, how would you be acting differently? If I were watching a videotape of your life, what would be different?

2. If a good friend saw you several months from now and you were more like the person you desire to be or your situation had significantly improved, what would this person see you doing differently?

3. What might some initial indicators be that would demonstrate you are headed in the right direction?

Phase 2

The client and the counselor construct a list of the behaviors that typify the "as if" person. Each one is evaluated individually to see if they are viable. The counselor may have the client rank the behaviors in order from the least difficult to the most difficult.

Phase 3

The client begins the process of enacting the first 2-3 behaviors in the coming week. The counselor works with the client to evaluate challenges and successes and through the consideration of adding addition, and more challenging behaviors.

Read the full article

Learning Outcomes

Upon completion of this Chapter, students should be able to:

1. Describe the Jungian concepts of the collective unconscious and the archetypes.

2. Utilize the results from the Myers-Briggs Typology.

3. Discuss Adler's concept of social interest.

Teaching

Ego Psychology

Work done within the vein of Freud (yet away and after him) is referred to as **Ego Psychology**. The focus was clear. Rather than researching the actions of the id and super-ego, well beyond our conscious control, the ego psychologists focused on the central role of the ego, or the self.

Anna Freud (1895-1982)

Anna Freud was the youngest of all of Freud's children and the only one to follow him into the field of psycho-analysis. Anna remained true to the basic tenants of Freud's work, expanding on them to include working with children and a further elaboration of ego defense mechanisms.

Anna did psychoanalysis with children taking into con-sideration their stage of development and limitations in language. She innovated with the process by introducing the use of toys and observing children in their own home.

The type of psychoanalysis developed by Anna Freud and others became the primary form that was introduced into America.

Anna Freud

Melanie Klein and Object Relations Theory

It is important to recall that when using the word "object" Freud was referring to any person, object, or activity that can satisfy an instinct (drive.) Object relations theorists focus on the interplay between these objects and the development of the personality.

Melanie Klein

One of the most important steps that need to be taken is the gradual break away from parental objects in order to become an independent human being. During the first six months of life, the mother is the most important object in the child's life. The type of relationship that is developed here, according to Klein, shapes relationships that the individual will have throughout their life.

Carl Jung

Freud once referred to Carl Jung as the the future heir of the world of psychoanalysis. Once their friendship disintegrated, Jung went on to develop his own model, analytical psychology, which was very opposed to many of Freud's ideas.

Relying on the details of his dreams to influence many of his decisions, Jung chose to study science, nature, and ultimately psychoanalysis. His interest, however, was in the unconscious, rather than the conscious mind.

Carl Jung

Jung had developed a professional relationship prior to his relationship with Freud. This may have made him less prone to the demands of absolute loyalty that Freud demanded of his followers.

Analytical Psychology

Analytical Psychology departs from Psychoanalysis in a number of ways:

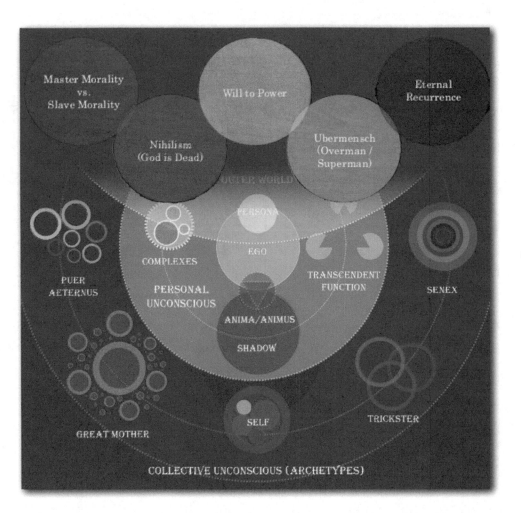

This image portrays the interrelationship between different archetypes and the personal ego in line with Jung's concept of the Collective Unconscious.

Visit this website to see what some of these symbols mean!

1. Sexuality is NOT the central theme.

2. Inner growth rather than social relationships was the focus.

3. For Jung, Libido was a generalized life force of which sexuality was only a part.

4. While Freud felt that his patients were victims of their past (or fantasies), Jung felt that our goals, hopes, and aspirations played significant roles as well.

The Collective Unconscious

With his focus on the unconscious, Jung proposed that there were two layers to the unconscious. One was our personal unconscious which is vey much like the unconscious self that Freud described.

The second level is the collective unconscious. It contains the cumulated experiences of previous generations, including our animal ancestors. These universal, evolutionary experiences form the basis of personality.

Archetypes

Archetypes inhabit the collective unconscious. These are innate determinants of mental life that dispose a person to act like their ancestors had acted in similar situations. Jung referred to the archetypes as the "gods" of the unconscious. Here are some of the standard archetypes:

1. **Persona** - this is the "mask" we wear when we are around other people and describe the person we want to be seen as in public.

2. **Anima and Animus** - puts for the notion that each person exhibits characteristics of the other sex. Anima refers to the female while Animus refers to the male qualities.

3. **Shadow** - this aspect of our personality represents the darker, more animalistic aspect of our personality.

4. **Self** - It contains the cumulated experiences of previous generations, including our animal ancestors. These universal, evolutionary experiences form the basis of personality.

Personality Types

According to Jung, the personality functions through six function:

1. **Introversion** - directs energy inwardly.
2. **Extroversion** - directs energy outside the self to others.
3. **Thinking** - a conceptual process that provides meaning and understanding.
4. **Feeling** - a subjective process of wighting and valuing.
5. **Sensing** - the conscious perception of physical objects.
6. **Intuiting** - perceiving in an unconscious way.

You might recognize some of these concepts if you have ever been exposed to the Myers-Briggs Typology. The fact is, the MBTI was developed based on Jung's concept of personality type.

MBTI

Katherine Briggs and her daughter Isabel Briggs Myers became fascinated with Jung's theories on personality and eventually added another dimension, judging or perceiving. Judging reflects a more controlled and planned out lifestyle where as perceiving is a more flexible and adaptive lifestyle.

The MBTI produces scores along 4 dimensions:

1. Introversion (I) vs. Extroversion (E)
2. Sensing (S) vs. Intuition (N)
3. Thinking (T) vs. Feeling (F)
4. Perceiving (P) vs. Judging (J)

The results produce a series of 4-letter sequences that correspond to a letter from each pair (as indicated above.) One combination might be INTP another may be ENFJ. The total number of possible combinations is 16. These constitute the 16 Personality types of Jung's theory!

The 16 Personality Types

Other Contributions by Jung

Much of scientific psychology rejects the work of Jung because he did not utilize controlled scientific experiments and had a tendency to interweave mystical and religion-based theories into his ideas. His work has still had a profound impact on the world of psychology.

1. Jung developed the word-association test still used in clinical settings today.

2. Personality structures such as introversion and extroversion (and the rest of those associated with the MBTI) remain important.

3. Archetypes and the collective unconscious continue to be intriguing notions.

4. He developed the notion of self-actualization which was later picked up by Abraham Maslow.

5. The concept of mid-life crisis was first established by Jung.

6. His work on the symbolism of dreams remains a profound work that contributes to the use of dreams in treatment today.

ISTJ Responsible, sincere, analytical, reserved, realistic, systematic. Hardworking and trustworthy with sound practical judgment.	**ISFJ** Warm, considerate, gentle, responsible, pragmatic, thorough. Devoted caretakers who enjoy being helpful to others.	**INFJ** Idealistic, organized, insightful, dependable, compassionate, gentle. Seek harmony and cooperation, enjoy intellectual stimulation.	**INTJ** Innovative, independent, strategic, logical, reserved, insightful. Driven by their own original ideas to achieve improvements.
ISTP Action-oriented, logical, analytical, spontaneous, reserved, independent. Enjoy adventure, skilled at understanding how mechanical things work.	**ISFP** Gentle, sensitive, nurturing, helpful, flexible, realistic. Seek to create a personal environment that is both beautiful and practical.	**INFP** Sensitive, creative, idealistic, perceptive, caring, loyal. Value inner harmony and personal growth, focus on dreams and possibilities.	**INTP** Intellectual, logical, precise, reserved, flexible, imaginative. Original thinkers who enjoy speculation and creative problem solving.
ESTP Outgoing, realistic, action-oriented, curious, versatile, spontaneous. Pragmatic problem solvers and skillful negotiators.	**ESFP** Playful, enthusiastic, friendly, spontaneous, tactful, flexible. Have strong common sense, enjoy helping people in tangible ways.	**ENFP** Enthusiastic, creative, spontaneous, optimistic, supportive, playful. Value inspiration, enjoy starting new projects, see potential in others.	**ENTP** Inventive, enthusiastic, strategic, enterprising, inquisitive, versatile. Enjoy new ideas and challenges, value inspiration.
ESTJ Efficient, outgoing, analytical, systematic, dependable, realistic. Like to run the show and get things done in an orderly fashion.	**ESFJ** Friendly, outgoing, reliable, conscientious, organized, practical. Seek to be helpful and please others, enjoy being active and productive.	**ENFJ** Caring, enthusiastic, idealistic, organized, diplomatic, responsible. Skilled communicators who value connection with people.	**ENTJ** Strategic, logical, efficient, outgoing, ambitious, independent. Effective organizers of people and long-range planners.

Alfred Adler and Individual Psychology

Adler is considered the first proponent of social psychology in psychoanalysis. His theory incorporates social interests.

Alfred Adler

Adler proposed the idea of social interests as a motivating factor of human behavior. He proposed that we have an innate potential to cooperate with others to achieve personal and societal goals. Unlike Freud's focus on the past, Adler felt that our perceptions of the future were a greater influence on us.

The next aspect of Adler's difference from Freud, and difference from many in his day, is worthy of quoting directly out of our text:

Another crucial difference between Adler and Freud was their views on women. Adler argued that there was no biological reason, such as Freud's concept of penis envy, for any alleged sense of inferiority women might feel. Adler charged that this was a myth invented by men to bolster their own alleged sense of superiority. Any inferiority women might feel resulted from social forces such as sex-role stereotypes. Adler believed in equality for the sexes and supported the women's emancipation movements of the day.

Inferiority

Adler supported the notion of a general sense of inferiority (or fear of it) as another motivating factor in human behavior. Inferiority feelings work toward the advantage of both the individual and society because it motivates a continual process of improvement. Failure to adapt and develop adequately can sometimes lead to the development of what he called an **inferiority complex**.

Adler referred to our general ways and behaviors for dealing with inferiority as our **style of life**. He felt that our style became fixed at about age five and was difficult to change after that point. Very optimistic, however, Adler also felt that our style of life had a lot to do with our ability to determine our own personality (very different from Freud) an ability he referred to as the **Creative Power of Self**.

Birth Order

Although many might not know that this concept arose from Adler, he is the one who developed our current notion of the influence of birth order on personality.

We have all heard about the impact of birth order on our personality! As the graphic above describes, first borns tend to be motivated and become leaders, youngest tend to be attention-seeking and fun, while the middle borns tend to feel left out and sometimes even lost.

Alfred Adler's work with families in the development of his Individual Psychology led him to engage in this very popular and compelling research. There is only one problem...it is not true.

What the Research Says...

The truth is, there are many, many factors that contribute to our personality and despite the compelling arguments about parenting different kids in order, there is very little evidence that birth order itself leads to specific types of personalities.

FIRST BORNS	MIDDLE BORNS	LAST BORNS	THE ONLY CHILD

FIRST BORNS	MIDDLE BORNS	LAST BORNS	THE ONLY CHILD
responsible	feels left out	uncomplicated	seeks approval
motivated	peacemaker	manipulative	sensitive
conscientious	social	seeks attention	leader
controlling	adaptable	self-centered	confident
cautious	people-pleaser	fun	center of attention
reliable	can be rebellious	social	mature for their age
perfectionist	independent	charming	conscientious
achiever	go-between	outgoing	responsible
leader			perfectionist
bossy			

Is Birth Order a Myth?

Personally, I find this lack of evidence to be sad. When I first got into Psychology, this was a very well-respected theory. Not only that, my own family upbringing taught me that this is true!

I have two brothers, and I'm the youngest. My family, Alan (oldest), Jim (middle), and me (youngest) can be pictured as the very example of Birth Order theory! You could replace pictures of Alan, Jim, and me in the graphic above and it would be a perfect match.

Not only that...my mom was an only child. She would have fit right in with that personality description as well!

"This just goes to show that even when we have personal experiences to draw upon, they are not enough to sustain scientific analysis.

Karen Horney

Horney was an outspoken woman among a field of outspoken men. She disagreed with many of Freud's concepts related to women.

1. In contrast to Freud's "Penis Envy" Horney stated that men are motivated by "womb envy" since they do have the ability to give birth.

2. Men attain womb envy and belittle and harass women because of it.

3. All people have the desire and potential to become decent (Freud felt that all humans were doomed)

Karen Horney

Basic Anxiety

Horney conceptualized the notion of basic anxiety, "the feeling a child has of being isolated and helpless in a potentially hostile world." Basic anxiety results from parental actions such as dominance, lack of protection and love, and erratic behavior. Anything that disrupts the relationship between parents and their children can bring about basic anxiety.

Neurotic Needs

In the presence of basic anxiety the child develops behavioral strategies for dealing with their parents. If these become fixed in their adult years, they become neurotic.

1. **The compliant personality**—one who needs to move toward other people, expressing needs for approval, affection, and a dominant partner

2. **The detached personality**—one who needs to move away from people, expressing needs for independence, perfection, and withdrawal

3. **The aggressive personality**—one who needs to move against people, expressing needs for power, exploitation, prestige, admiration, and achievement.

Individuals may create an idealized self-image that is a facade. This "mask" may keep the individual with neurotic needs from fully understanding themselves.

Humanist Psychology

Partly in response to the determinism that is embedded in Freudian-based psychology and Behaviorism, the notion of Humanist Psychology emerged. A precursor to today's Positive Psychology, Humanists espoused the values related to free will, emotional health, kindness, and generosity.

This movement was profoundly influenced by two of the most famous psychologists in history, Abraham Maslow and Carl Rogers.

Abraham Maslow

Maslow's main contention, much in opposition to the prevailing Behaviorist mentality of the day in the US, was that each of us possesses an innate tendency toward self-actualization, or the fulfillment of our potential.

Abraham Maslow

Maslow began to study the lives of persons he felt were self-actualized and concluded that they all had any number of the following traits:

1. An objective perception of reality

2. A full acceptance of their own nature

3. A commitment and dedication to some kind of work 4. Simplicity and naturalness of behavior

4. A need for autonomy, privacy, and independence

5. Intense mystical or peak experiences

Maslow's hierarchy of needs is based on a theory of motivation. Individuals must essentially satisfy the lower deficiency needs before they become focused on satisfying the higher Being needs. Beyond even the Being needs there is something more, a state of transcendence that ties all people and the whole of creation together.

6. Empathy with and affection for all humanity

7. Resistance to conformity

8. A democratic character structure

9. An attitude of creativeness

10. A high degree of what Adler termed "social interest"

However, he postulated that we had to first satisfy lower needs in order to prepare for self-actualization. This was the beginning of his now famous Hierarchy of Needs.

Hierarchy of Needs

Of all the work that Maslow did, none is more famous than his **Hierarchy of Needs**. Similar to Rogers, Maslow felt that we are all drawn toward self-actualization. However, in our journey toward self-actualization there is a hierarchy of needs that we need to meet first.

The basic premise of the Hierarchy of Needs is that as we are being drawn toward self-actualization (and beyond, in what Maslow referred to as "transcendence") we are driven to satisfy more basic, lower-level needs. They exist in sequence, and for the most part, we can't go on to satisfy the next need until the previous one is complete. (Later in life Maslow rejected this rigid structure, but none-the-less, the hierarchy serves as a good summary of basic human needs.)

Self-Actualization and Fourth Force Psychology

As part of the birth of Positive Psychology, Maslow engaged in the study of people he felt had achieved self-actualization, led self-actualized lives, and/or had achieved transcendence. This focus on those who lead very fulfilling lives is the hallmark of Positive Psychology. Keep in mind that much of the world of Psychology is based upon the study of those who are not doing well! Not many healthy, adjusted people go to see the Psychologist!

The book summarizes the characteristics of a self-actualized person very well. As much as we would like to think we are all these things, truly self-actualized individuals are very rare. But, we do know when we are in the presence of one! These personality characteristics not only manifest but they seem to manifest regardless of the situation the person is in!

At the time of his death, Maslow was entering a new field of study, **Transpersonal Psychology**, a field he felt was the next step in the world of Psychology (having called Humanistic Psychology as the Third Force Psychology.

"I should say also that I consider Humanistic, Third Force Psychology to be transitional, a preparation for a still "higher" Fourth Psychology, transpersonal, trans-human, centered in the cosmos rather "than in human needs and interest, going beyond humanness, identity, self-actualization, and the like...These new developments may very well offer a tangible, usable, effective satisfaction of the "frustrated idealism" of many quietly desperate people, especially young people. These psychologies give promise of developing into the life-philosophy, the religion-surrogate, the value-system, the life-program that these people have been missing. Without the transcendent and the transpersonal, we get sick, violent, and nihilistic, or else hopeless and apathetic. We need something "bigger than we are" to be awed by and to commit ourselves to in a new, naturalistic, empirical, non-churchly sense, perhaps as Thoreau and Whitman, William James and John Dewey did. (Maslow, 1968)"

Carl Rogers

Person-Centered

Carl Rogers did not "father" the field of Humanistic Psychology (Maslow did that, as we will discuss later), but Rogers was a clinician. He felt he needed to find a new method for helping his clients that was more effective and more inline with his own thoughts. As he developed his clinical approach, much like Freud, he developed a unique theory of personality that explained why it was effective.

Carl Roger's approach to therapy emphasized the individual. Originally he coined the term "client-centered" but then later restated it as "person-centered" and the modern concept of Person Centered Psychotherapy (still in practice today) was born. In contrast to the very "hands on" approach of psychoanalysis, person centered approaches were very "hands off."

Carl Rogers

The goal of the clinician is to simply facilitate the changes the client wants to make. They do this largely through active listening and restraining themselves from being too directive. This fit very well with Taoist philosophy that Rogers had been exposed to in his travels.

1. *If I keep meddling with people, they take care of themselves.*

2. *If I keep from commanding people, they behave themselves.*

3. *If I keep from preaching at people, they improve themselves.*

4. *If I keep from imposing on people, they become themselves.*

Lao Tzu, c600 BC

As with the Humanist movement that Maslow spearheaded, Roger felt that the one basic drive in all individuals is to self-actualize. To Rogers, self-actualization was the tendency to move forward, toward greater maturity, or self responsibility.

The Self

In Roger's definition of the self, he makes several points that include his thoughts about the experiential field (the unique sum of our experiences, circumstances, emotions, thoughts, and attitudes), our self-actualizing tendency (our motivation to move forward), and our self. Rogers felt that by engaging in our experiential field we can have experiences that modify the self and move us toward greater self-actualization. He called this personal power and rested it right in the person (as opposed to a doctor.)

The Development of the Personality

When a child is born, it has an innate drive to self-actualize. As a child becomes self aware it develops a need for **positive regard**. If the parents provide **unconditional positive regard** the child will move forward. If the parents, instead, have **conditional positive regard** (positive regard will only be forthcoming under particular circumstances), then the child with develop **conditions of worth**. The child will then begin to act in accordance to these ongoing external demands rather than living his or her own life.

Throughout life, we behave in different ways and evaluate if it is in **congruence** with our perception of our self. We experience **congruence** and we feel good about our behavior when there is a match and we feel **incongruence** when we behave in ways that are not true to our self.

Structure of the Personality

In this section I will be covering Roger's theory of the structure of the self, but I've also added a component to it. There are, at all times, three versions of the self that coexist. These are defined as follows:

1. The **True Self** is the person you really are. This is the one that resides and acts in your unique

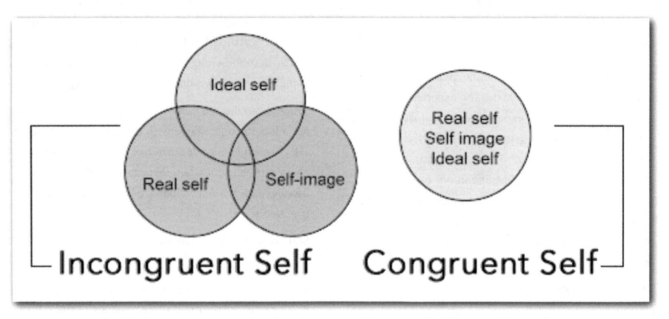

In this image you can see that there is crossover between the different selves in the incongruent self, but total integration of the three selves in the congruent self.

experiential field. It is the true self that only you know.

2. The **Ideal Self** is the sum of the person you would like to be.

3. The **Social Self** or **Self Image** is the form of the self that you express in public and in society. It is the "you" that everyone else sees.

In one application of Roger's concept of congruence we can see this process as an integration of these three selves until they are very similar. The congruent self would be the individual who has a true, ideal, and social self that are all the same! In truth, this is very difficult as we strive to be better (ideal self) and we are often in circumstances that call on us to be a different self (social self).

In my experiences I have seen this increased degree of congruence manifest particularly in the elderly population. As we age, we become more aware of our limitations)and may mitigate our ideal self goals) and we become less concerned with what others think about us (social self) so we are just ourselves! Any of you that have elderly relatives that "say it like it is" know exactly what I'm talking about!

The innate drive to self-actualize is sometimes difficult to understand. Western thinking tends to look for tangible answers as to what this means (success, wealth, health, the good life, etc.) Eastern philosophies have been dealing with this concept for much longer and have a very different perspective. To that way of thinking there is a natural order of life, the universe and our place in it.

"So whether we believe in God, Tao, an eternal Self, a mortal Self, or merely an actualizing tendency, for thousands of years there has been the belief, amongst many people, that our lives are about more than just being alive for a limited period of time. And it is in the recognition and acceptance, indeed the embracing, of that something more, even if we can't conceive it in our conscious mind, that we find and live a good life."

Social Relationships

Unfortunately we are often a relatively poor judge of our own congruence. Having relationships with people we can trust is vital to our development as a person. (I need not mention the relation this has to Looking Glass Self!)

Rogers felt there were numerous relationships that we engaged in that would benefit us in this way, but that none was as vital as marriage. Rogers spent a lot of time researching what constitutes a happy and successful marriage.

1. **Dedication and Commitment** - when the thrill of the relationship can seem to disappear, what will keep the relationship together? A deep dedication to the other person and a commitment to working through changes.

2. **Communication** - it is particular vital to communicate persistent feelings and to own these feelings rather than project them on to the other person.

3. **Dissolution of Roles** - society provides many expectations for relationships and the roles within them. Healthy relationships define their own.

4. **Becoming a Separate Self** - a "living" relationship is composed of two individuals who continue to develop their own selfhood. As each person becomes more real and integrated, they bring this continual process into the relationship and contribute to the growth and development of the other.

I will leave the discussion regarding person-centered therapy to the discussion in the textbook. However, you should know that Roger's approach, his concepts of unconditional positive regard, congruence, and empathy have had the most impressive impact on the practice of psychotherapy today. There are hardly any practitioners who do not credit Roger's for fundamental aspects of their approach to helping others.

Assessment

Chapter 14 Discussion

Discuss Adler's concept of social interest. Discuss your thoughts on his concept of an innate potential to cooperate with others to achieve personal and societal goals.

Chapter 14 Quiz

1. Describe the Jungian concepts of the collective unconscious and the archetypes.

Chapter 14 Assignment - MBTI

Purpose

The purpose of this assignment is to familiarize yourself with one of the most famous applications of Carl Jung's theories, the Myers-Briggs Type Inventory, or the MBTI.

The MBTI is one of the most famous personality tests in the world. A key advantage of the MBTI is that there are really no "negative" personality types. The instrument is used widely to gain insight into how a person processes information, makes decisions, and works with other people.

Skills and Knowledge

You will demonstrate the following skills and knowledge by completing this assignment:

1. Complete the 16 Personality Types test.

2. Research aspects of your typology related to how you interact with others.

3. Administer the test to another person.

4. Engage in a discussion as to how your personality types interact with one another.

5. Write a title page and paper in a word processor.

6. Upload the paper to the assignment drop box.

Task

In this assignment you are going to use the 16 Personality Types test to assess your own personality and the personalty of someone close to you.

Step 1

The 16 Personality Types

Step 2

Complete the test and review your results. Feel free to look up other websites and resources related to the types, there are many, many of them!

TypeLogic Website

Step 3

Using the test, conduct a personality assessment of another person close to you. Look up their results.

Review the results that both of you have and document the discussion you have about your differences and similarities and what these mean for your relationship.

Step 4

Write up a paper documenting this project.

Criteria for Success

Use the rubric below as a guide to this assignment.

Title Page   10 points
Standard title page with name, date, course, college name and the name of the assignment.

Your Results   25 points
Include the letter combinations and a brief description of your personality. You may have more than one!

Other's Results   25 points
Include the letter combinations and a brief description of their personality. They may have more than one!

Discussion   25 points
Summarize your discussion about each other's type and what it means for your relationship. Be specific

Mechanics   15 points
Spelling, syntax, and organizational structure of the paper. Clear and organized.

Contemporary Developments in Psychology

15

Attention

7 Digit Telephone Numbers

When telephones started the way in which you got in touch with someone was to ring into the switchboard and ask to be connected. Later, with the addition of rotary dials with numbers and letters, we could place a call directly by dialing in their mnemonic code...a combination of letters and numbers that was easy to remember.

Elston Electric Company
MORE INFO

As more telephones became into use, Bell Telephone had to find a way to code the new numbers and make the easy to remember. They had a plan in mind, but they needed some scientific validity to pull it off.

Bell Telephone reached out to Harvard professor George Miller who was doing ground-breaking work on memory. Miller's article "The Magical Number Seven, Plus or Minus Two: Some Limits on our Capacity for Processing Information" was just what they were looking for!

It was decided that phone numbers, separate from area codes, would consist of no more than 7 digits.

453-5438

If the area code was included, it would be put in parentheses.

(207) 453-5438

A few of Miller's principles are at play here. First the 7 digits, which is the average number a person can process (according to Miller). Second, they chunked digits together in order to enhance memory, and put the area code in parentheses to activate other parts of the brain to help retain those.

Our phone number is the result of extensive research in Cognitive Psychology!

Read the full article!

Learning Outcomes

Upon completion of this Chapter, students should be able to:

1. Describe how changes in thinking in Physics opened the door for Cognitive Psychology to emerge.

2. Define "ecological validity."

3. Discuss the concept of Artificial Intelligence.

Teaching

Cognitive Psychology Beginnings

Throughout this study we have examined various schools of thought regarding psychology and watched them come into being, attract followers, splinter into sub-groups based on disagreements, and then, in most cases, disappear from the mainstream. Each of these processes, however, have left their mark on our current thought in psychology. Our present is decidedly built upon the foundation of each of these movements, even if we have some pretty old bricks in that foundation.

In the 1970s it can be said that "Psychology found its mind" (after losing it for a while) and the pendulum has swung a bit back to a focus on the internal processes of thinking, cognition. Whether we attend to this internal world or not has largely been the battle lines of many of the theories we have explored so far. Some saw it as a waste of valuable research (behaviorism) while others felt the internal world was pretty much all there really was (existentialism).

Jean Piaget (1896-1980)

A young Jean Piaget

Piaget was a brilliant scientist with an early interest in mollusks about which he published his first academic paper at age 10.

His keen scientific mind allowed him to objectively observe his own children and develop one of the most important theories regarding cognitive development, **genetic epistimology** or, the "genesis of how we come to know things."

Although his work was not immediately accepted in the United States because of the influence of Behaviorism, he later attained the acclaim that he deserved.

Physics Leads the Way (Again)

Physics has long been the role model for Psychology. At this point in history the world of Physics was being turned upside down by Albert Einstein, Niels Bohr, and Werner Heisenberg. The new physics discarded the need for total objectivity and the complete separation of the observer in science. Absolute knowledge itself was deemed unattainable, and the subjective perspective became all we had to work with. Although the founding of the Cognitive school of thought does not have a specific individual (like Behaviorism has Watson), there are some leading early thinkers.

George Miller (1920-)

One of the most famous contributions to Cognitive Psychology from Miller was his article titled "The Magical Number Seven, Plus or Minus Two: Some Limits on our Capacity to Process Information." You learned a bit about this in the Attention section of this chapter.

The amazing thing about this article is that it dealt directly with cognition itself, a study of how we think and remember things.

Ulric Neisser (1928-)

Neisser's first academic appointment was, fortunately, at Brandeis University where Abraham Maslow was the Chair of the Department. Maslow was already moving away from the strict Behavioral model, so it was an ideal place for Neisser to explore a new direction. His book *Cognitive Psychology* ushered him in as the "Father" of Cognitive Psychology.

Neisser became frustrated with the new field of Cognitive Psychology, however, with its reliance on experimental studies. He insisted that the field should have ecological validity. By this he meant that the results should be generalizable outside of the laboratory.

The Computer Metaphor

Machines are built by humans and thus they are a reflection of the creator. By understanding the creation we can understand the creator (and this has all sorts of metaphysical implications!)

The modern metaphor for the human mind is the computer. Much of what Cognitive Psychology is concerned with is exemplified in the operation of modern computers. As computers have developed, their similarities to the human mind continue to intrigue us.

Artificial Intelligence

The computing genius Alan Turing created the "Turing Test" as a way for us to determine if true Artificial Intelligence exists.

The interrogator [the subject] has two different "conversations" with an interactive computer program. The goal of the interrogator is to figure out which of the two parties is a person communicating through the computer and which is the computer itself. The interrogator can ask the two parties any questions at all. However, the computer will try to fool the interrogator into believing that it is human, whereas the human will be trying to show the interrogator that she or he truly is human. The computer passes the Turing Test if an interrogator is unable to distinguish the computer from the human.

At this point there is no evidence for real AI despite our machines being very smart and quick and able to perform all manner of tasks.

Cognitive Psychology Today

Cognitive Psychology today can be characterized in the following ways:

1. Focus on the process of knowing rather than merely responding to stimuli.

2. Focus on how the mind structures and organizes information.

3. Believe that people actively and creatively arrange the stimuli that they experience.

Other areas that are meaningful focal points of Cognitive Psychology include:

1. Cognitive Neuroscience

2. Introspection

3. Unconscious Cognition

4. Animal Cognition and Personality

Evolutionary Psychology

Evolutionary theory is still a persistent presence in Psychology. Evolutionary Psychologist embrace the following:

1. All psychological mechanisms at some basic level originate from, and owe their existence to, evolutionary processes.

2. Darwin's theories of natural and sexual selection are the most important evolutionary processes responsible for creating evolved psychological mechanisms.

3. Evolved psychological mechanisms can be described as information-processing devices.

4. Evolved psychological mechanisms are functional; they function to solve recurrent adaptive problems that confronted our ancestors.

Assessment

Chapter 15 Discussion

Discuss the concept of Artificial Intelligence. Look up apps and websites associated with this topic. Reflect your research in your discussion.

Chapter 15 Quiz

1. Describe how changes in thinking in Physics opened the door for Cognitive Psychology to emerge.

2. Define "ecological validity."

Special Assignments

Article Review

Purpose

The study of history, particularly the study of the history of a field like Psychology, is filled with names, dates, and places. But sometime, we lose the frame of reference for the sequence of events. Sometimes we learn things in a particular sequence but it is not clear that two successive events were happening at the same time.

Also, as a study of human behavior, connected to other sciences in the world, the history of world events plays a role in formulation of ideas. We can see clearly in this course how the World Wars impacted the development of Psychology.

Skills and Knowledge

You will demonstrate the following skills and knowledge by completing this assignment:

1. Explore literature in the History of Psychology.

2. Select an article from the provided list and obtain it through the library or other sources.

3. Summarize the major findings of the article.

4. Summarize the importance of the study in terms of modern psychology.

5. Include a "References" page as the last page in your document with the single article in APA format.

6. Write a title page and paper in a word processor.

7. Upload the paper to the assignment drop box.

Task

The following list contains articles that have been found to explore the important issues associated with studying the history of psychology. Consider these examples of how specific articles from the list have explored these issues.

<u>Showing how events in psychology's history can be fit into a broader historical context</u>

- showing why spiritualism was popular in late nineteenth century America (Coon, 1992)

- placing Goddard's work in the context of early twentieth century concerns about immigration (Gelb, 1986)

<u>Illustrating the dangers of presentist thinking</u>

- explaining the reasons why the APA's reaction to the Clarks' research, which contributed to Brown v. Board of Education, was minimal

- explaining the reasons for the apparent anti-Semitic phrasing found in some of Woodworth's letters of recommendation (Winston, 1996)

<u>Challenging the typical student belief that if it's in the text book, it must be true</u>

- the political reasons for the structure and content of Boring's famous text (O'Donnell, 1979)

- the errors in portraying Pavlov's apparatus (Goodwin, 1991)

<u>You cannot understand modern psychology without understanding history</u>

- animal rights ("antivivisection") at the turn of the twentieth century (Dewsbury, 1990)

- the notion that experiments produce causal conclusions, but correlations don't (Winston, 1990)

<u>Historians rely heavily on archival materials</u>

- all of the articles on the list

Here is the list of articles you can choose from for this assignment:

Benjamin, L. T., & Crouse, E. M. (2002). The American Psychological Association's response to Brown v. Board of Education: The case of Kenneth B. Clark. *American Psychologist, 57,* 38-50.

Benjamin, L. T., Jr., Rogers, A. M., & Rosenbaum, A. (1991). Coca-cola caffeine, and mental deficiency: Harry Hollingworth and the Chattanooga trial. *Journal of the History of the Behavioral Sciences, 27,* 42-55.

Burnham, J. C. (1972). Thorndike's puzzle boxes. *Journal of the History of the Behavioral Sciences, 8,* 159-167.

Coon, D. J. (1992). Testing the limits of sense and science: American experimental psychologists combat spiritualism. *American Psychologist, 47,* 143-151.

Dewsbury, D. A. (1990). Early interactions between animal psychologists and animal activists and the founding of the APA committee on precautions in animal experimentation. *American Psychologist, 45,* 315-327.

Fuchs, A. H. (1998). Psychology and "the Babe." *Journal of the History of the Behavioral Sciences, 34,* 153-165.

Furumoto, L. (1992). Joining separate spheres—Christine Ladd-Franklin, woman-scientist (1847-1930). *American Psychologist, 47,* 175-182.

Gelb, S. A. (1986). Henry H. Goddard and the immigrants, 1910-1917: The studies and their social context. Journal of the History of the Behavioral Sciences, 22, 324-332.

Goodwin, C. J. (1991). Misportraying Pavlov's apparatus. *American Journal of Psychology, 104,* 135-141.

Goodwin, C. J. (2005). Reorganizing the Experimentalists: The origins of the Society of Experimental Psychologists. *History of Psychology, 8,* 347-361

Green, C. D. (2003). Psychology strikes out: Coleman R. Griffith and the Chicago Cubs. *History of Psychology, 6,* 267-283.

Harris, B. (1979). Whatever happened to Little Albert? *American Psychologist, 34,* 151-160.

Leahey, T. H. (1992). The mythical revolutions of American psychology. *American Psychologist, 47,* 308-318.

McReynolds, P. (1987). Lightner Witmer: Little-known founder of clinical psychology. *American Psychologist, 42,* 849-858.

O'Donnell, J. M. (1979). The crisis of experimentalism in the 1920's: E. G. Boring and his uses of history. *American Psychologist, 34,* 289-295.

Nicholson, I. (1998). Gordon Allport, character, and the 'culture of personality", 1897-1937. *History of Psychology, 1,* 52-68.

Pickren, W. (1997). Robert Yerkes, Calvin Stone, and the beginning of programmatic sex research by psychologists, 1921-1930. *American Journal of Psychology, 110,* 605-619.

Richards, R. J. (1983). Why Darwin delayed, or interesting problems and models in the history of science. *Journal of the History of the Behavioral Sciences, 19,* 45-53.

Rutherford, A. (2003). B. F. Skinner's technology of behavior in American life: From consumer culture to counterculture. *Journal of the History of the Behavioral Sciences, 39,* 1-23.

Smith, L. D. (1992). On prediction and control: B. F. Skinner and the technological ideal in science. *American Psychologist, 47,* 216-223.

Sokal, M. M. (1981). The origins of the Psychological Corporation. *Journal of the History of the Behavioral Sciences, 17,* 54-67.

Winston, A. S. (1990). Robert Sessions Woodworth and the "Columbia Bible": How the psychological experiment was redefined. *American Journal of Psychology, 103,* 391-401.

Winston, A.S. (1996). "As his name indicates": R. S. Woodworth's letters of reference and employment for Jewish psychologists in the 1930s. Journal of the History of the Behavioral Sciences, 32, 30-43.

Criteria for Success

Use the rubric below as a guide to this assignment.

Title Page   10 points

Standard title page with name, date, course, college name and the name of the assignment.

Summary of Article   20 points

Without copying the abstract and based upon reading the ENTIRE article, you are to summarize the findings of the article (at least two paragraphs.)

Application   40 points

Reflect on the content of the and align it to one of the important issues outlined in the task description.

- Showing how events in psychology's history can be fit into a broader historical context.

- Illustrate the dangers of presentist thinking.

- Challenge the typical student belief that if it is in the textbook, it must be true.

- You cannot understand modern psychology without understanding history.

- Historians rely heavily on archival materials

APA Citation of the Article   20 points

Add a References page and write out the APA format citation of the article you are reviewing. All aspects of APA format must be observed.

Mechanics   10 points

Spelling, syntax, and organizational structure of the paper. Clear and organized.

History Timeline

Purpose

The study of history, particularly the study of the history of a field like Psychology, is filled with names, dates, and places. But sometime, we lose the frame of reference for the sequence of events. Sometimes we learn things in a particular sequence but it is not clear that two successive events were happening at the same time.

Also, as a study of human behavior, connected to other sciences in the world, the history of world events plays a role in formulation of ideas. For example, we can see clearly in this course how the World Wars impacted the development of Psychology.

Skills and Knowledge

You will demonstrate the following skills and knowledge by completing this assignment:

1. Research the details of the life of a psychologist.

2. Report the results of this research in chronological order.

3. Research specific histories of world events that encompass the dates of the life of the psychologist.

4. Contribute to the construction of a class-wide graphic timeline.

Task

Each student will select a single psychologist (or other person of interest from the history of Psychology) as a subject. You will research the individual's biography and document the following significant features of their lives:

1. Date of Birth and Location.

2. Places they have lived.

3. Educational milestones.

4. Publication and/or presentation milestones.

5. Family events (marriage, divorce, kids, etc.)

6. Death (if applicable)

In addition to the timeline of the individual, you will also construct a timeline of significant social and cultural events during the time. Your research into the social and cultural history will include:

1. Specifics in the history of Europe.

2. Specifics in the history of the United States

3. Specifics in the history of the country in which the person resides.

All of this information will be submitted as a paper as outlined in the rubric below.

As a class, we will be combining the information from all the participating students and constructing a visual timeline (more information on that aspect of the project will be discussed in class.)

Criteria for Success

Your assignment will be graded using the following rubric:

Title Page — 10 points

Standard title page with name, date, course, college name and the name of the assignment.

Timeline for Psychologist — 40 points

Timeline includes:

- Date and place of birth
- Places they have lived
- Educational Milestones
- Publication and/or presentations milestones
- Family events
- Death (if applicable)

Timeline for Europe — 20 points

Relevant social and cultural events.

Timeline for US — 20 points

Relevant social and cultural events.

Mechanics — 10 points

Spelling, syntax, and organizational structure of the paper. Clear and organized.

Here is a list of the Psychologists you CANNOT do because they have already been done.

- William James
- Lewis Terman
- Ivan Pavlov
- Albert Bandura
- Sigmund Freud

Made in the USA
Coppell, TX
27 January 2023

11807139R00157